HEALTH SOLUTIONS FOR
STRESS
RELIEF

Rebalance your natural stress-resilient body chemistry with stress-busting foods, fast stress rescues, and 140 clinically proven stress-management techniques

DR. JAMES ROUSE

For Debra, Dakota, and Elli—the girls of my life

WE **INSPIRE** AND **ENABLE** PEOPLE TO IMPROVE
THEIR LIVES AND THE WORLD AROUND THEM

We're always happy to hear from you. For questions or comments concerning the editorial content of this book, please write to:

Rodale Book Readers' Service

33 East Minor Street

Emmaus, PA 18098

Look for other Rodale books wherever books are sold. Or call us at (800) 848-4735.

For more information about Rodale magazines and books, visit us at

www.rodale.com

Editor: Christine Bucks

Interior Book Designer: Joanna Williams

Cover Photographer: Gaiam

Interior Photographers: Ron Derhacopian (poses), Mitch Mandel (food), and Gaiam (all others)

Layout Designer: Donna Bellis

Copy Editor: Erana Bumbardatore

Product Specialist: Brenda Miller

Indexer: Nanette Bendyna

Rodale Organic Living Books

Executive Editor: Margot Schupf

Art Director: Patricia Field

Content Assembly Manager:
Robert V. Anderson Jr.

Copy Manager: Nancy N. Bailey

**Library of Congress
Cataloging-in-Publication Data**

Rouse, James.
    Health solutions for stress relief : rebalance your natural stress-resilient body chemistry with stress-busting foods, fast stress rescues, and 140 clinically proven stress-management techniques / James Rouse.
        p.   cm.
    Includes index.
    ISBN 1–59250–151–6 paperback
    1. Stress management.   2. Stress (Psychology) I. Title.
RA785.R68   2003
613.7—dc22   2003014506

**Distributed in the book trade
by St. Martin's Press**

2 4 6 8 10 9 7 5 3 1 paperback

Contents

Acknowledgments

I would like to acknowledge Spirit and its guiding light and inner voice that has inspired me to follow my heart, act with compassion, love with zeal, and live with gratitude and humility for the gift of life.

This book represents a co-creative culmination of energies and expertise provided by colleagues, friends, family, and loved ones. Special thanks to my parents—Mom, Dad, Gail, and Bob—for establishing a foundation for me to build my dreams upon. To my sister and brother, Tamara and Bryan, I am grateful for your hearts and spirits, which you express with integrity and love. A heartfelt thank-you to all of my clients and patients who have continually inspired me through their commitment to healing and wholeness.

I am grateful for the experience, expertise, and encouraging enthusiasm of Kerry Eielson, whose energy and dedication to excellence allowed for my thoughts to be represented so well in the pages of this book.

I am grateful for the opportunity to create with the gifted people at Rodale, Christine Bucks and Margot Schupf, and for having the benefit of their editorial expertise. I also wish to acknowledge fellow mind mapper Ron Derhacopian for his photographic excellence.

Thank you to Howard Ronder for your creative eyes and heart; to Andrea Lesky for your passionate persistence in bringing the workouts to life; to Jirka Rysavy for sharing your courageous heart and vision with the whole world. To Lynn Powers, my friend and mentor, thank you for leading with your heart with passion, purpose, and impeccable grace.

Finally, I wish to acknowledge and dedicate this book to the greatest blessings and teachers in my life: my wife, Debra Jeanne, and my two most beautiful girls, Dakota and Elli. I appreciate your love, hugs, and laughter, as you have given me the experience of having heaven on earth.

Your Road to Balance

Of all the patients I see in my office every day, 9 out of 10 are there because of unmanaged stress and its impact on their physical or emotional health.

You, too, may be here—having picked up this book—because stress has gotten out of control and is negatively affecting your life. You may have reached a point where the pressure of stress has so changed you that you hardly recognize yourself. Your patience has flown the coop. Your coping skills have eroded. You find yourself not knowing how to approach changing times, and you feel that you just can't deal anymore.

Chronic stress, when not channeled properly, will compromise life on every level—including your capacity to dream and strive for goals. For many of us under unrelenting stress, the driving desire in our lives becomes just to be safe. So we tiptoe through life, trying to avoid whatever stresses us out.

But what we need to come to terms with is the fact that stress is a part of *any* life. Stress doesn't have to be a bad word. Even exciting things like new jobs and fulfilling relationships can create stress. When managed correctly, it's not necessarily a negative influence. This book is not about avoiding stress. It's about harnessing it and making it work for you.

Consider this: Stress becomes a problem when you let it—when you allow yourself to be subject to the conditions you live in. Most people tend to live life *outside-in*. We look at what's going on around us and then live according to those external realities or principles. We are shaped by others' realities.

There is a saying that expresses one of the greatest means to overcome stress: "Be in the world and not of it." The overlying goal of this book is to help you live *inside out*. If you live inside out, the formative forces in life come from within. Your motivating drive will come from your heart, not from external pressures. Your choices will reflect what's inside you, who you are, and what's best for you, for your health, and for furthering (or finding) your purpose. Strive to be able to say, "My world is an expression of me," instead of, "I am an expression of the world."

Working On an Inside Plan

If you want a less stressful life, become a less stressful person. Create a life that transcends conditions. Live inside out. Find tools for peace that can't be taken away. Learn to make proactive lifestyle choices. Live a life by design, not by default.

My approach to treating stress is based on holistic, naturopathic medicine, which aims to treat the cause of disease through positive lifestyle practices and natural medicine instead of using drugs to treat symptoms. Practitioners of naturopathy believe that when a person's physiological and spiritual balance is restored and maintained, his body is better able to prevent illness and cure itself of disease.

In applying the principles and practices outlined in this book, you will adopt a healthy lifestyle that will allow you to make decisions and resolve problems from a place of centeredness, peacefulness, patience, hope, and abundance, thereby reducing the amount of stress you absorb on any given day.

The core values of a lifestyle favoring healthy stress management are outlined in Part One: The Hows and Whys of Stress. Scattered through this section are solutions you can reach for at any time to help buffer your response to stress.

Concrete lifestyle practices to help channel and alleviate stress in the long run and in emergency situations are detailed in Part Two: Solutions for Stress. This section answers the question, How can I be breathing, moving, thinking, and expressing my life so that I deal better with stress on a daily basis? In this part of the book, you'll find ways to help you alleviate stress through meditation, exercise, and diet. Meditation, exercise, and diet work together to cushion the body chemistry so that your body can absorb the stress response when it occurs, and they create a strong foundation for a life lived to its max.

I've presented my suggestions for stress solutions in an A.M./P.M. format. By scheduling healthy routines into every morning and every evening, you will create what I like to call bookends for self-care. Marking this time for yourself every single day is the only way to reach a successful life of balance. Instead of giving yourself more to do, have a slot of time at the beginning and end of every day to do less. Make this your time for being well and doing things that make you happy and healthy.

On Your Mark . . .

Embarking on the road to balance and well-being can be a solo act. In our society of frantic doing, where no one gets accolades just for being, taking downtime every day may not be looked at favorably. If you're not sure the people in your life would support what you're doing, don't tell them. It may be a good idea to keep it to yourself initially so your efforts aren't sabotaged. If people need to know why you're not available, tell them you're working on a project for the next month. Give yourself the time and space you need to create new, healthy habits with deep roots. Take an at-home vacation or retreat: Don't answer your phone, don't check your e-mail, don't make plans—just relax and care for yourself.

This is a learning experience—less about will power and more about willingness. It can take years to truly master stress, so please go easy on yourself. One of the greatest modern American stressors is perfectionism. This program is not another stressor to add to your life. Think of it as another course in the life school. This is not a place where you arrive fully packaged and ready to go. You come here to learn. Move away from perfectionism and toward excellence. Be flexible and open to learning. This book will take you through the first step of the process today and head you through the journey of finding peace.

(signature)

Part One: The Hows and Whys of Stress

1

Causes of Stress

What's stressing you out?

Social challenges are the most commonly recognized stressors. Many of these social triggers probably seem pretty obvious: having a bad day at work, getting a flat tire, or even simply having to wait in a long line at the grocery store. But situations that we perceive as positive can also cause stress. A new job, though exciting, can be anxiety provoking. Any new role in life, no matter how enriching, such as marriage or parenthood, will increase your overall stress level if you don't manage new challenges well.

One social stressor that often slips under the radar, though, is others' expectations. An enormous amount of stress comes from living your life the way you think it's "supposed" to be lived. You react in the manner that you were taught is correct, or you make decisions because they are the "right" choices. Acting based on others' desires often means sidelining your own dreams. In the long term, this whittles away at your happiness and sense of fulfillment—two great barriers against stress. There's also a social responsibility, especially in our country, to have the right face on all the time. Our culture places great emphasis on looking happy, seeming to be on top of everything, and acting like we've got it going on, even when that's not true. We are expected to continue to push ourselves and not show the stress in our lives, no matter what.

This, however, doesn't mean that you need to live each day wallowing in your own misery. What it does mean is that you need to accept what's going on in your life—and once you do that, you can start to improve it. It's incredibly difficult to manage stress if you deny it exists. This is one of the reasons it's such an epidemic in America. What a relief it is to say, "Wow. I have a full life, and I'm totally maxed. This is hard!" As soon as you can acknowledge that you've got a lot going on and that it's hard to handle, you can recognize the richness of your life and all the things you have to be thankful for.

Keep in mind that social challenges aren't the only triggers for stress. The environment (both internal and external) and its effect on your body also play roles in stress.

Stress can be caused by anything in the environment that challenges your body, including factors such as extreme cold or heat. In Chinese medicine, such forces are called External Pernicious Influences (EPIs). EPIs are considered to be some of the greatest potential stressors to your immune system. Though this is believed by many in the West to be an old wives' tale, Chinese healing practitioners still strongly believe that EPIs account for many colds, flus, and—by way of an overworked immune system—disease in general. In places where consistently nasty weather is an issue, this belief is also held true. You'd be hard pressed to find an Irishman who doesn't think it's a bad idea to sit in the way of a draft.

Other environmental factors that heavily tax the body are pollution, toxins, and allergens, which are prevalent in today's world no matter where you live. These triggers greatly stress the liver, as well as the immune system. When the body is faced with extra toxins to process, the liver goes into overdrive and simply can't keep up. The more environmental stressors you're exposed to, whether they're from pesticides or air pollution, the greater the toll on your liver and your health.

Because you're bombarded with stressors from the environment, many of which you have little control over, it's extremely important to do what you can to minimize how these stressors affect you on the inside. Enjoying nutritious, organic foods; breathing deeply; and exercising are very powerful tools to help combat stress on the body.

Self-neglect also taxes your body. Poor eating habits, lack of exercise, and improper breathing are, in the long run, as detrimental to your system as anything else. And while your exposure to some stressors may not be under your control, taking care of yourself is.

HEALTHY AND UNHEALTHY STRESS

Not all stress is bad for you. The distinction between healthy and unhealthy stress can actually be more about how you handle life's challenges than it is about the challenges themselves. For example, a new job is not bad for your health, but stressing out and worrying about it is.

Most of the time, we choose to be stressed out. We invite stress in and allow it to fester or explode. An unmitigated stress response will get out of control. All too often, the size of the reaction far outweighs the significance of the source of stress. For example, at some point in your life you may have gotten as upset over something as insignificant as a parking ticket as you would have if you'd found out that your spouse had had an affair. This is an overreaction, and it's quite common. Overreacting is something we as a society allow, or even encourage.

Some of this overreaction may have to do with how many stress hormones are already coursing through your veins when the ticket arrives. The stress of the ticket is like rubbing salt in a wound, and you reach a breaking point. But still, the initial perception of the ticket as something stressful, instead of as a mild inconvenience, is a choice. You allow it to start, and you can stop it from happening.

CONTROLLING THE SUBJECTIVE

Stress can be objective or subjective. Objective stress comes from an unanticipated fright, like when you accidentally set off a department store alarm, a mouse runs across your kitchen floor, or you have a fender-bender. Objective stress is due to physical perceptions of danger and is much less common today than subjective stress. Subjective stress is brought on by intellectual perceptions and often has to do with one's state of mind; it's about how you see an event. Subjective stressors include anxiety over a promotion, the first day at school, divorce, or moving. These things aren't bad news to everyone; after all, one person's liberation is another's nightmare. Subjective stress is under your control.

Unhealthy stress also comes from worrying about "What ifs." What if I get fired? What if I miss that car payment? What if my teenager gets sick and misses his college entrance exam? Living in the past is a source of stress, too: If you experience something traumatic and replay that event over and over, there comes a time when the playback is no longer therapeutic, but instead is a source of unnecessary stress.

ACUTE AND CHRONIC STRESS

In addition to being healthy or unhealthy, stress can also be acute or chronic. Acute stressors are things that cause disruptions in your day-to-day plans, like traffic jams, lost keys, and computer crashes. Impending events, such as a wedding, vacation, or move to a new home, can cause acute stress, too. While acute stress *is* taxing, it's usually not unhealthy.

Chronic stress, on the other hand, can be pervasive and debilitating. Chronic stress comes from larger, weightier issues that wear on you day in and day out. Present, long-lasting challenges such as financial instability, a family illness, a poor diet, lack of exercise, poor self-image, overwork, unhappy relationships, an unfulfilling career, and global political insecurity will damage your health over the long run if you do not do what you can to neutralize their physiological effects. Persistent emotional issues and the baggage that you carry, such as an unhappy childhood or internalized anger or grief, are also chronic stressors and are equally debilitating.

Chronic stress is a real danger. Prolonged stress keeps us in an imbalanced chemical state that we can actually become accustomed to. Our sense of drama becomes desensitized; we become unable to recognize that we are under stress at all. We fuel existing stress levels for another rush. We become attracted to the buzz of stress hormones, and eventually we can get addicted to them. The detrimental effects of this can't be overstated.

PHYSICAL AND MENTAL TOLLS

Stress affects your body both physically and mentally. On the physical side of things, stress is a major factor in disease. An imbalanced body chemistry resulting from chronic stress results in everything from lower energy and fatigue to sickness and even premature death. Stress is such a significant factor in poor health that as much as 90 percent of doctors' visits are due to stress-related illnesses.

Over time, stress highly impacts a person's immune system and emotional well-being. Studies have linked stress with alcoholism, asthma, cancer, digestive problems, headaches, heart disease, memory loss, obesity, osteoporosis, and more. Stress can wreak havoc on the body's most vital systems, impacting neurological, immunological, and cardiovascular functions.

On a mental level, stress can create anxiety, depression, lack of confidence, and loss of a sense of purpose and direction. It can lead to situations of spiritual deprivation where we begin to face life from a place of scarcity. We feel we don't have enough—not enough money, not enough possessions, not enough love, help, energy, compassion, or time.

Physically, mentally, and emotionally, we become incapable of living fully. Working from this position in life can affect everything, including our jobs and relationships. We may act strangely around those we love and treat them with impatience or ignorance. Or we may isolate ourselves from our communities. Stress can make us all islands. We're together in being stressed out, but in our stress we become disconnected. This kind of isolation further decreases our ability to handle stress.

Stress is truly corrosive. As it wears us down, we become less and less able to defend ourselves from it.

THE GOOD NEWS

As you become able to manage stress, you will thrive. You will be able to grab stress with both hands and subdue it. This book will give you the roadmap to negotiate stressors of all kinds: big and small, chronic and acute, subjective and objective. By following this program, no matter what comes at you—even if it's something you've never seen before, something catastrophic that you've never considered—your body and mind will be fortified and you will be able to work through it.

The solution is in your hands. Make the decision now to manage your response to the world. Step back, and make a pledge to learn about your stress.

2

Your Body on Alert

How does your body react to stress?

We usually think of "stressing out" as an emotional problem. But the way our bodies react to stress is actually chemical—a biological process. The stress response is a prehistorically designed defense system intended to spur us into action and thereby protect our lives from lions, tigers, bears, and other life-threatening forces; this is why it has been dubbed the "fight or flight" response.

An all-out danger isn't necessary to tip off the stress response, though. As I discussed in Chapter 1, the body interprets any change in its environment as a potential concern. The brain sends a message to the body to prepare for something different, and prepare it does. Everything in the system rallies around this change in case it leads to something menacing.

So what actually happens physiologically in response to stress? For starters, stress causes a major fluctuation in body chemistry by releasing a flood of chemicals and hormones into the bloodstream. The adrenal glands react to the alert by releasing epinephrine (adrenaline), which makes the heart pump faster, providing blood to areas (such as arms and legs) necessary for response to the stressful situation. The lungs work harder, as respiration increases to supply necessary oxygen to the heart, brain, and muscles. Blood vessels dilate or constrict. The adrenal glands also release extra cortisol and other glucocorticoids, which help the body convert sugars into energy. Blood sugar levels increase as the liver dumps stored glucose into the bloodstream. Nerve cells release norepinephrine, which tenses the muscles and peaks the senses to prepare to react, while simultaneously reducing production of digestive secretions.

TOO MUCH CORTISOL

The rush and burn of stress begins with a set of chemicals, namely adrenaline and glucocorticoids like cortisol—hormones that provide the body with energy in the form of sugar and fat so it can exert itself. Adrenaline is released in response to acute stress. Its release in the body should be very short-lived. When an event becomes a chronic stress situation, glucocorticoids like cortisol take over. Cortisol, in and of itself, is beneficial to the body. Chronically elevated levels of cortisol are anything but.

Cortisol is a steroid hormone produced by the adrenal gland in response to stress. It regulates the body's metabolism of glucose, protein, and fatty acids. As a control board for these elements in the body, it has a very significant, essential physiological role. Cortisol regulates mood and well-being, immune cells and inflammation, blood vessels and blood pressure. It also supports healthy maintenance of connective tissues like bones, muscles, and skin. Cortisol is critical to keeping us well and alive. We don't want to suppress its production in the body, we just want to have the right amount. The body is also engineered to produce

RELAXATION THROUGH IMAGINATION

After you've experienced an acutely stressful situation, you should exercise or practice some kind of relaxation technique. If you don't have the opportunity to exercise, use your imagination to help disengage the stress response before it turns into a chronic situation. Practice breathing slowly from your diaphragm. Envision and invite relaxation through picturing a soothing vista, memory, or event that promotes peace of mind.

cortisol to help us move around and relieve stress. Cortisol wouldn't be a problem if every time we got bad news we moved around and encouraged our cortisol levels to return to normal.

In excessive amounts, cortisol is what gives us that buzzing feeling. If it's not burned off, it produces the tight, wound energy you feel during crisis mode, as opposed to the refreshing flow of energy you get after going for a nice, long walk.

The effects of chronic cortisol elevation are many and varied. It can make you fatter because all the extra amino acids and sugar in your bloodstream that haven't been burned off will be stored in your body as fat. Elevated cortisol levels also encourage cravings for sugar and carbohydrates. Excess cortisol also appears to interfere with the body's ability to absorb calcium and can therefore lead to osteoporosis. It suppresses energy and exhausts the adrenal system. Chronic levels of this steroid also curb dehydroepiandrosterone (DHEA) in the body—the "mother hormone" responsible for the production and regulation of estrogen, progesterone, and testosterone. Because of these hormonal fluctuations, cortisol can inhibit sex drive. Perhaps the most significant problem caused by unrelentingly high cortisol levels in the body is a greater susceptibility to disease.

Imbalanced cortisol levels can suppress the immune response and downshift the activity of the body's killer cells, our primary defense against viruses, bacteria, and cancer. When a body is functioning with high cortisol levels, not only does it fail to defend itself against disease, it actually invites disease in. High cortisol levels can result in autoimmunelike tendencies, contributing to susceptibility to allergies, asthma, arthritis, colds, flu, and frequent upper respiratory infections. It can also increase the likelihood of skin problems and digestive disorders. Remember, stress is defined as any challenge to the body, including disease. By making you more susceptible to illness, stress clears the road for greater stress, and a truly vicious cycle begins.

YOUR BRAIN ON STRESS

Your brain is starved when it's under chronic stress. As high cortisol levels send all the energy, nutrients, and amino acids to your skeletal muscles and limbs so they can run or do battle, very few of these nutrients remain available for your brain, challenging your brain's glucose levels. Subsequently, your brain, which uses glucose as food, loses out and begins to shut down. When your brain lacks food, it can't do a good job of supplying your body with energizing and feel-good hormones such as dopamine and serotonin, both of which can help restore physiological and emotional balance. These nutrients feed the brain's neurotransmitters, imparting an ability to focus, remain calm and happy, sleep well, and crave the right foods. Without the nutrition necessary to support the building blocks for healthy thinking or high energy levels, our ability to manage stressful situations is greatly impaired.

When the brain is starving, we face challenges with depression, forgetfulness, and anxiety. In the long run, this means we might be more susceptible to serious disorders such as dementia and memory loss. In the short term, stress messes up brain waves.

The stress response does not facilitate rational or intellectual activity of any kind. When your life is threatened, you don't have time to intellectualize and put things in perspective, so this lack of rational thought isn't a problem. Instinct takes over. In dealing with contemporary stress, however, we need to be able to function thoughtfully. When your brain can't think of ways to move out of stress, high-level, insistent stress only becomes more chronic as you become less able to think of solutions to it.

The brain operates on electrical impulses, such as alpha waves and beta waves. When we're stressed-out, we move into a beta-dominant state, which can confuse our thinking and make us feel frenetic and mentally scattered. In a beta frame of mind, you experience an inability to think straight. When you're in a beta state, your thought process is very fragmented and your memory is poor. That's why when you're under stress, you can't recall a number you know like the back of your hand. You see an old friend and you can't remember who he is because your brain is not there. Beta waves make it very difficult to restore balance.

When you move into more meditative states, which decreases cortisol and supports healthy neurochemistry, your brain moves into an alpha state. This is a relaxed and alert condition that allows you to be "on." Your thinking is clear. An alpha brain allows you to be crisp, attentive, present, and focused. Intellectually and spiritually, you tend to be much more centered. This is the state you will learn to nurture through dietary choices, exercise, breathing practices, and the maintenance of an objective distance from your struggles and a positive outlook on your life.

WHAT DOES IT ALL MEAN?

In the clutches of the stress response, the body perceives a threat to its survival. Although today's stressors have become less life threatening than they were several hundred years ago, the body responds with the same intensity that it did back then. It will do everything it can to protect itself, even if the stressor is abstract, such as stress over money or lack of time, or when it's entirely in the realm of your imagination. For example, if you indulge in dark daydreams about having your apartment robbed or losing a loved one, your body will experience changes at a chemical level that will put it in fight-or-flight mode.

Stress chemicals compel the body to move. The thing is, we don't—usually because we can't. When we're stressed while sitting in front of a computer, at a meeting, or in a traffic jam, we can't fight or flee. We perceive an annoyance; our bodies perceive danger and overreact. It's a good thing not to fight, but it's a great thing to run and move after a stressful event. Unfortunately, rather than run, we ruminate. And when we ruminate, the problems begin. All the hormones, glucose, and fatty acids that get dumped into the blood stream for use by the arms and legs just sit there, saturating the body with stress hormones.

This is why stress is harmful. The stress response in and of itself is not a bad thing. Your body is doing what it's supposed to do, and it does it very well. But we don't do with it what we should be doing. We don't move. And that lack of movement, in addition to our diet, sedentary lives, and habits such as shallow breathing create a physiological environment that favors a trigger-happy stress response. Because of today's lifestyle, many people are chronically chemically imbalanced. On top of that, we mismanage the stress response, tapping into it and overreacting to trivial inconveniences, further disrupting balance.

Later in this book we'll work on two fronts to fix this instability: You'll learn to taper your reaction to stressors and create a chemical equilibrium in your body that's better able to absorb the stress response when it necessarily occurs.

3

Moving Toward Empowerment

How do you deal with stress?

In the first two chapters of this book, we looked at what causes stress and how our bodies react to stress. But how do we actually deal with stress—particularly in a society where "the rules" dictate that we can't let anyone see us sweat?

Gender is one determining factor in how we deal with stress. In general, men deal with stress by using more physical, primal outlets—such as participating in contact sports—than women do. And men who don't take to their heels often escape through watching sports; there's a very primal release to all the shouting and shaking of fists during football games and boxing matches.

Physical outlets don't offer men an intellectualization of what's stressing them out, nor do they provide perspective, emotional distance, or possible solutions to their problems. Going to a

ENHANCE YOUR BELIEF SYSTEM

Some people turn to a higher power when trying to deal with stress. And as part of a larger strategy, faith can be a vital part of stress management. But alone, it may do little to solve problems or strengthen the body, and it can fall short of being a proactive response. Some belief systems encourage followers to deal with stress by not dealing with it at all. And sometimes the way we practice our religion may not nurture spirituality, even if it has that potential. This is an opportunity to really get clear with yourself. Do you derive a sense of spirituality and faith from your religion that extends to how you face each day? Is your belief system enough to help you deal with today's world? Do you apply your religion to your life? Make it a goal to enhance your belief system, bring it alive, and apply it to your life on every level.

soccer game for some primal screaming is a release, but without contextualization, there's no long-term reduction in stress levels; the response stays the same. The masculine response can actually feed further release of stress hormones into the system, which is why male stress hormones are running amok. Men die more often from heart disease than women, a factor that has been linked to the way men handle stress.

Women, on the other hand, tend to react the opposite way. Although many women do exercise for stress relief, most women talk it out with friends, family, or a therapist, or write in a journal. Women discuss and intellectualize stress. While this may initially seem like a good way to handle stress, by itself it may not be a great deal healthier over the long run than the male reaction. Talking yourself in circles offers no physical release.

The right balance, of course, would be a combination of the two reactions, using both physical outlets and intelligent conceptualizing to work through problems and channel excess energy.

WHY NOT POP A PILL?

In society today, prescription medications such as antidepressants and antianxiety drugs are also seen as ways to cope with stress. These drugs are designed for short-term use and can be very effective when used correctly and under the supervision of a licensed therapist or physician. Their purpose is to help you get over a crisis and be able to handle everyday life in the meantime. (Of course, they are also effective as long-term solutions for people who suffer from mental illness.)

Many Americans, however, are on long-term, unsupervised courses of mood enhancers and emotion alleviators. A multimillion dollar industry has been built on never getting to the source of one's stress, on smoothing the surface of things to maintain the appearance of normalcy. Medication alone doesn't get to the cause of a crisis or reach a permanent solution. Used as a disguise for one's current emotional makeup, medications are, in my opinion, a cop-out. The backlash of this is an inevitable (though not inherent) inability to deal with problems on one's own, guaranteeing a future need for such "solutions."

ADOPTING A HEALTHY LIFESTYLE

The first step toward dealing with stress is to acknowledge what's stressing us out. This process takes courage. It's a trust walk to actually look at these things, investigate them, and reflect upon why we make the choices we do.

I prescribe a program that addresses the basic principles of sustainable well-being by using a mind-body approach that builds patients' physical and mental foundations with nutrition, fitness, and spirituality. By focusing each patient on how he feels, I eventually uncover the larger life issues that need to be resolved. To truly master stress, it's necessary to develop a sense of purpose in life, to arrive at a feeling of peace with work and relationships. My overall goal is for each of my patients to reach balance in every area of life.

The best way to deal with stressors and handle them better is to prepare for them physically, mentally, and emotionally. To do this, you need to adopt a healthy lifestyle that allows you to make decisions, resolve problems, and face situations from a place of centeredness, peacefulness, patience, hope, and abundance.

Faith in Action

When it comes down to it, the single thing that makes the biggest difference in terms of dealing with stress is the faith that everything will be okay. Learn to trust that life will not let you freefall until you hit the pavement. "Faith in action" is basically this ability to move through the world with a sense of spiritual confidence that no matter what comes, you will have the resources in your heart and soul to deal with it. This is my call to action for you: Think about how you can take your faith and put it in a proactive place. How can you use it to move through the day with confidence, a sense of resiliency, and also a sense of purpose?

Faith has many paths and many definitions. The faith I'm talking about here is a kind of personal faith—faith in yourself and your own life. Faith in action is a personal belief in your ability not only to overcome challenges but also to accept all life has to offer and thrive in the world. The program in this book builds faith in action. By following its principles and practices, you will have the resources—nutritional, physical, and spiritual—to deal with what comes your way.

Many people claim not to have faith because they are not religious. Spirituality is an instinct we are all born with and which we can express in many ways. I don't believe it's possible to lose faith, but it *is* possible to stifle it. Taking care of yourself is the first step toward reviving and expressing your faith in life. The greatest blessing of faith is that it is dynamic. One's belief system is always tempered, challenged, and then reaffirmed in beautiful ways. Allow your faith to be ever-evolving. No matter what happened yesterday or even five minutes ago, you have an opportunity to resurrect and reclaim your faith, to come back to it and let it replenish your spirit.

Regardless of where you are on the continuum of faith, embrace the idea that creating a routine of self-care may build faith. For example, walking or doing yoga followed by eating a balanced breakfast in the morning should be non-negotiable; if they are, you will make begin to make inspired, spirited choices. When you move and eat well, you think well. And when you think well, you move out of scarcity thinking and into abundant-minded consciousness, where you become an inspired human being. All of a sudden, life is possible again.

Know What Makes You Nuts

Sometimes we get so enmeshed in our craziness that we can't see the forest through the trees. We don't think mainlining a pot of coffee is crazy. We don't think sleeping three hours a night is unusual, tossing and turning the rest of the time. We don't think getting a stomachache over a typo in a report is unnecessary.

Unchecked, the stress response can all of a sudden get out of control because we let the floodgates open.

Stress management begins with an intellectual intervention. Awareness is the first step toward having a mindful reaction to trials and tribulations. Start keeping a stress journal so you can objectively study what causes stress in your life. Keeping such a record can help you realize what is not normal in your life and help you refuse to accept it anymore. For example, when you're up at night, what do you mull over? What pushes your buttons, and why? You may realize that getting upset over certain things is just habit; you've outgrown the problem, but you respond the same way as before. What can you do with that information? When you're on your morning commute, are you just driving or are you thinking about the confrontations you might have and how you'll respond? On the way to your child's soccer game, are you worried about how he will perform? What is the common theme on days when you have bad headaches? What is the recurring subject when you pick a fight with your partner? Write down all the things that drive you nuts—your bank account, a sibling, broken promises, a stain on your favorite new jacket, low self-esteem—whatever it is, no matter how small it may seem, get it down on paper.

Next, ask how stress affects you. If your answer is, "I get stressed," ask the deeper question: What's underneath that stress? Fear and foreboding? Anger? Grief?

TAKE THE TIME

One of the greatest stressors is time, or lack of it. People feel they don't have enough room in their schedules to make positive change in their lives. Take a look at what you do with *your* time. You don't have to go to a spa or religious retreat to experience healing. You don't need three weeks of open space to begin to care for yourself. Find the time in every day. You *do* have time.

A week contains 168 hours. If you work 50 hours a week and sleep 50 hours a week, you have 68 hours a week to do with as you wish. I'm asking you to take 7—give yourself at least 7 hours a week for healing, happiness, and well-being. Record your schedule every day, including how much time you spend eating, sleeping, talking on the phone, e-mailing, and flipping through channels. Find a way to save just 1 nonnegotiable hour a day for yourself. All I ask from you is 30 minutes in the morning and 30 minutes at night. This 60 minutes a day could transform the quality of your day and of your life.

People respond to stress in very different ways; some become almost manic under pressure, while others just cave in and become depressed. Are you uptight? Have you lost your sense of humor? What are your physical symptoms of stress? Do you get bad colds after a very busy time? Do you suffer from headaches on bad days? Does worrying keep you up at night? Many people cope by not coping at all. In stressful times, do you eat, drink, fight, watch television, shop, or zone out?

Once you've identified your stressors and how stress affects you, you can begin to anticipate stress. Look for patterns, and prepare yourself. Many stressors happen on a regular and predictable basis. Credit card statements come at the beginning of the month. Traffic usually gets jammed at the same time of the day. Strategy meetings are scheduled for every Tuesday. Maybe you feel stress every time you see a certain person, deal with a specific task, or encounter a specific kind of news story. Once you identify your stress-inducing triggers, you can prepare to deal with them mindfully and proactively. Draw up your stress calendar, make up your mind to stay calm, and let what would be repetitive stressful situations roll off you like water off a duck's back.

You also need to build a supportive body chemistry. Even if you're not ready or don't yet have the courage to look hard at what is out of whack in your life, at least do this. Through focusing on physical fitness, optimism, and balanced nutrition, you will be able to build a healthy body—and once your body is healthy, you'll have the wherewithal to take a look at the stressors in your life and figure out how to deal with them.

RULES TO LIVE BY

Make a conscious effort to adopt the following life rules, and your efforts to deal with stress will be off on the right foot.

Rule 1: Be present. As I've previously said, much of stress is imagined. It originates in the realm of your mind; you invent it. Stress is not necessarily the end of an old relationship; stress is what you do while worrying whether or not you will ever love again and whether or not you made the right decision. Stress is the refusal to accept things as they are. When you worry that negative events in the past mean you will have negative events in the future, it produces stress. As far as your body is concerned, stress, whether real or imagined, is cause for alarm. The most effective solution to unnecessary mental and emotional baggage is also the most obvious: Focus on the here and now.

Rule 2: Be proactive. A denial of the present can lead to a vicious cycle of self-neglect. As the present gets laid by the wayside, so do healthy habits. When you don't value the present, routine goes out the window and mental energy is not invested in constructive, positive thoughts. Taking care of yourself and your health roots you firmly in the present and leaves you less at the mercy of hypothetical problems and situations. Moving your body, eating low-stress foods, and thinking positively also keep the levels of stress hormones in your system to a minimum. With less cortisol coursing through your system, you are less likely to slip into a full-throttle stress response over a lost sock.

Rule 3: Be accountable. Get real! When subjective stress is not invented, it's often invited. Take responsibility for the degree to which you get stressed out. We tempt many of the unnecessary stressors in life just by making uninformed decisions or acting thoughtlessly. Consider the consequences of your actions, and ask whether they are worth the outcome. If you use your credit card for an extravagant purchase, you know as well as I do that it will need to be paid for with real money. If, in three weeks when the bill arrives, you're surprised at the bottom line, your lack of realistic thinking is an issue you need to come to terms with. Love what is. Be straight with yourself and with life. This does a lot to decrease stress.

Rule 4: Be thrifty with your emotions. This is a hard one for a lot of people who have grown accustomed to a high-drama existence. When everything is a really big deal, your perception of your own significance and the significance of your problems balloons deceptively out of perspective. A gentle, frank criticism made by a friend fires up your temper. You lose it over a malfunctioning cell phone the same way you would if something really horrendous happened. Emotions are for people and life, not for money, red tape, or parking tickets. Save your emotions for where they enrich your life, where you can learn and grow from them. Channel your emotions with discretion. Save your feelings for things that matter, and make your experience in life more poignant. It's your choice. See it, accept it, get annoyed if you have to, and move on.

Part Two: Solutions for Stress

4

Mind Over What Matters

Is the glass half full?

Shifting to positive thinking is vital to proactively solving stress problems. And positive thinking does more than solve daily difficulties and give you a greater capacity to enjoy each day (as if that's not enough!). Optimists live longer. They have greater cardiovascular health; a reduced risk of cancer and other diseases; lower rates of depression, anxiety, and obesity; and stronger immune systems.

Pessimism is a double-edged sword in that pessimism is a product of stress that creates even more stress. The good news, however, is that you can learn to be optimistic—it's within your power to change your mindset. Being stressed out and having negative reflexes can become habits. Mindfulness (being consciously aware of your reaction to challenges) can stop the pessimistic reaction before it starts. Exercising positive thinking can change your emotional reflex to be one that assumes the best.

We have between 60 and 90 thousand thoughts a day, close to 90 percent of which are old, recycled, automatic thinking. You want less stress? *Think* less stress. If you're caught in a web of tension, pressure, and impossibility, weave a new one of hope and enthusiasm. When you create new thoughts, you will have an opportunity to recreate your life.

BENEFITS OF MEDITATION

My goal with this book is to initiate new thinking and bring your body back to balance. Meditation is one way to accomplish just that. Meditation includes any way you integrate awareness and consciousness into every activity, such as by breathing deeply or using visualization and affirmation techniques.

Meditation does not require 30 minutes, special clothes, privacy, and a mat. The ability to meditate is like having a mobile phone. You can make a call anytime, anywhere. Meditation works on many levels to reverse the stress response. In terms of body chemistry, it cultivates a balanced state in the brain by supporting essential neurotransmitters. Meditation lowers blood lactate and decreases anxiety, reduces blood pressure, lessens cortisol, and moves the body into a hypometabolic state that allows it to use oxygen more efficiently. In a meditative state, everything moves into a place of balance. From this state, it's easier to nurture a proactive, motivated, and energetic approach to life.

Meditation is an opportunity for your body and brain to both step back. An overextended mind is a stressed-out mind. We are a culture of overdoers who take pride in being able to keep several balls in the air at once. We simultaneously do business, eat, drive, and write a to-do list. We watch the news while we study. We read or talk on the phone while we exercise or listen to the radio; we eat breakfast and talk on the phone while getting ready for work. Trying to do too many things at once can lead to a very scattered sense of being and to feeling overwhelmed and disconnected. When you step out of that active doing mode by meditating, your brain doesn't have to perform—it can take time to rest.

Another benefit of using meditation to deal with stress is that it develops objectivity, which can stop a panicked reaction before it starts. Awareness is the key to mastering your stress response. People who meditate and do yoga tend to notice and then make

TAKING BACK CONTROL

Meditation brings the focus to the here and now and encourages truth, accuracy, and acceptance. Present-moment awareness is one of the best ways to retrain your thought processes. A focus on your breath or on one thought or image can interrupt negative patterns by making you aware of them. It imparts a sense of control to that moment. One of the greatest stressors is the scary feeling that you are out of control, or that a situation is out of your control. Taking time to control your breath and discipline your mind reinforces that you are, in fact, managing the situation, you do have options, and you will find a solution. The same goes for establishing a morning and evening routine that allows for self-care, including the opportunity to map out what you want each day to be like and then work to achieve what you've planned. It puts a measure of control back in your life. You'll learn to see every moment, every action and reaction, as an opportunity to start fresh.

adjustments to difficult situations before they get stressed out. They are proactive and empowered under stress. People who don't take advantage of those kinds of mind/body practices are typically great reactors. As soon as they get the initial sense of anything uncomfortable, they fly into major stress mode, becoming irrationally enraged at a red light or at someone who won't move out of the passing lane. This is a tragic waste of time and energy—two human resources we all want more of.

Use the yogic and mind/body principles in this book and apply them to daily experiences. Stop, notice, and breathe before you react. Don't allow yourself to be rushed. Take the time to look for windows of opportunity. When faced with a challenge, don't make a habit of panicking. Instead, ask yourself, Is this really worth getting worked up about? Often, you'll discover that it's not.

You'll find it's a great relief when every day is not an adventure in red-alert scenarios—when you can live peacefully, rationally, and intelligently, no matter what's going on in the world.

Breathing Fully and Deeply

"Take a deep breath and count to 10." It's one of the oldest tricks in the book for dealing with a stressful situation, and yet one of the most underused. We have forgotten how to breathe properly—and not just when we're under pressure. Many of us actually neglect to breathe properly every day. We should breathe slowly and in a relaxed manner, using the whole torso to take in oxygen and letting the belly rise and fall with each breath like a bellows. Instead, we confine respiration to our collarbones. This cheats the body of its most essential need: oxygen.

Poor posture, lack of mindfulness, and (surprise, surprise) stress are the greatest culprits contributing to shallow breathing. Rounding your shoulders and letting your chest cave in, which happens when you don't sit or stand with an elongated spine, crushes your lungs and doesn't allow them to expand with each breath. Poor posture also doesn't allow room in your abdominal cavity for your diaphragm to drop and make more room for your lungs. On top of that, when you're nervous or anxious, you may go into a posture of self-defense, clenching your stomach and chest muscles. You hold tension in your back and shoulders. This constricts lung capacity. The key to allowing your body to breathe deeply is not just to focus on your breath and correct your posture, but also to allow your body to soften, to be in a more open and receptive mode.

While it's natural to take short, shallow breaths under stress, it's also the worst thing you could possibly do. Inefficient breathing initiates the stress response all by itself. The control boards for both respiration and the fight or flight response are located in the limbic system of the brain, and they are very closely connected functions. Our bodies interpret short breaths as a first-level response to danger, whether danger is present or not. Any time we begin taking shallow breaths, our bodies— which don't respond well to oxygen deprivation—think that we're stressed.

The physical consequences of shallow breathing are many. It encourages higher levels of blood lactate (which produces feelings of anxiety) and increases the likelihood of sodium retention, which can cause hypertension. Nine out of ten Americans will experience hypertension during the course of their lives. By contributing to high blood pressure, shallow breathing can possibly be a factor in kidney disease, heart disease, and stroke. These are major killers. By making us breathe poorly, among other things, stress is a catalyst for many challenges to longevity.

The most effective solution to shallow breathing is using your lungs to their fullest capacity. Breathe deeply. Doing so reverses damage done by breathing feebly: Slow, deep breaths lower blood lactate levels, put a halt to excessive production of cortisol, bring the brain to an alpha state, and can lower blood pressure. They also support levels of beneficial neurotransmitters such as serotonin and dopamine.

BELLY BREATHING

Practicing this technique on a regular basis will help you develop proper breathing skills that will help you deal with stressful situations.

To begin, sit or lie in a comfortable position. If possible, undo the waist of your clothing so that your belly isn't constricted. Relax the muscles in your chest and abdomen. Close your eyes and place your left palm directly on your belly button, fingers facing sideways. Cover your left hand with your right hand, lining your palm up with your navel again and interlacing your thumbs. Feel the heat of your hands on your belly. Inhale deeply and slowly through your nose, letting your belly inflate to its fullest, then letting your chest expand, and finally letting your back fill with air. When you can't inhale anymore, gently and slowly exhale. Repeat 10 to 20 times. For 3 extra breaths, inhale as deeply as you can, deeper than you did for the first 10 or 20 breaths, and release. Slowly open your eyes and think of something that makes you very happy.

So take 5 minutes every hour to breathe really deeply. This is great for productivity. By lowering cortisol, breathing properly helps your brain to initiate a wonderfully relaxed, but not sedate, state that allows for focus and concentration. Work on your breath during an important meeting and you will be more present, focused, and alert. In terms of everyday life, by fortifying your mind with adequate oxygen, you will enjoy a sharper ability to make the right decisions for your health and happiness.

Visualization and Affirmation

Think of visualization as using your imagination to help transform your life. Find a quiet place where you can get into a comfortable position, either sitting or lying down. Calm your breath by breathing slowly and deeply, in and out through your nose. When you sense that your mind and body are beginning to relax, imagine your life exactly as you'd like it to be. See each relationship, work situation, health challenge—or whatever is meaningful to you—and hold on to that image. Then think of a positive affirmation, such as, "I am full of energy and vitality, and each day my life becomes effortlessly more joyful and spontaneous." Affirmations are powerful because they set in motion a change that begins in your heart and mind—a change that can alter your self-image.

Repetition is key to visualization and affirmation, so practice these things daily, if not several times a day.

BREAKING THE PATTERN OF PESSIMISM

While meditation (including breathing properly), visualization, and affirmation all help to combat stress, the following suggestions also help combat stress by breaking the pattern of pessimism that so often accompanies and perpetuates stress in our lives.

Think about what you're saying and what it really means. Watch the adjectives you use to describe your prospective experiences—they can literally cast a spell on you. Saying "I'm scared," or "I'm nervous," before an interview will only perpetuate those feelings. Instead, channel that energy into something positive. Say "I'm excited," or even "I have no idea what to expect. The possibilities are awesome." Saying or even just thinking that something could go wrong will increase the chances that it will.

Surround yourself with positive props. We allow what we surround ourselves with to determine who we become. When we see an image, it elicits a thought. If that thought is positive, it starts to lay the framework for positive thinking and proactive living. But if we put ourselves in front of the daily newscast about fire, murder, and the economy, it can create a negative impression on our psyche, which can lay the foundation for a pessimistic way of interacting with the world. Ask yourself: What do you allow to imprint in your mind, your soul, your heart? What inspires you? What makes you feel joy in your life? Put images or reminders of those things all around you. Photos of beautiful places, quotes by inspired thinkers, books that made your imagination soar, mementos from loved ones, lists of your achievements—all these things can put you in an entirely new place, emotionally. Place them in an area where you spend a considerable amount of time (your office, your car, your kitchen, or even your bathroom) so you're constantly reflecting on and being reminded of the things that make you feel good.

Create a "To-Lose" List. It's time to lighten your load. Look at all the things that are absolutely not necessary in your life, and let go. You know what they are: Certain relationships, television shows, unhealthy habits, and old routines are keeping you in a lackluster life of pressure. Happy people who get involved with unhappy people lose themselves. There is an energy around positive people and practices that can do a number of good things for your sense of balance. As an exercise in gratitude, get rid of the things in life that bring you down. Do a toxic-people cleanse. Do a media fast. Be choosey about what information you deal with on a daily basis. Put yourself in places that feed your heart. This really requires a lot of initiative. As you begin to simplify your life, you will be surprised to discover who or what doesn't support you. In the process of finding what *does* support you, you will begin to get in touch with and fulfill your higher purpose.

Seek your higher purpose. A self-actualizer is someone who becomes aligned with his higher purpose. On an emotional level, stress has a lot to do with unfulfilled dreams. When someone's life is not aligned with his heart, a chronic dissatisfaction and self-limiting apathy set in. Think of your life's direction. Where would you like to be? What is your biggest, wildest dream? What gives you more life? Define irrevocable happiness. What are the things that give you joy that can't be taken away?

Create bookends. Often, the only time we have some measure of being in charge of our lives is early in the morning and right before bedtime at night. These are times when we can create our own rituals. Starting today, begin to give yourself an extra 30 minutes in the morning and the evening. Start your bookend before you even get out of bed by performing 20 deep belly breaths. Then allow yourself to come into the day gently, with soft light, gentle music, soothing tea, and a good book. Then take an invigorating walk, meditate, or do yoga. Similarly, do the same kinds of activities for at least 30 minutes before bed each night. Make sure to dim the lights, as this prepares your body chemistry for sleep. Use the principle of bookends as a hug, one arm in the morning and another arm in the evening wrapping around your day, holding you safely, holding you in a place of accountability, and holding you in a place of possibility.

5

Exercising Your Body and Mind

How balanced is your approach to fitness?

Movement is one of the most beneficial ways to alleviate tension, be it physical or emotional. A sedentary life compounds stress. Butterflies in your stomach before a big event or feeling totally exhausted after a busy week is your body's way of telling you to get up and move. And if you did, you'd feel a lot better.

Of course you're already familiar with many of the health benefits you get from exercising. Exercise is essential to maintaining a healthy weight, bone density, cholesterol level, blood pressure, and metabolism. But regular exercise is also one of the greatest cushions for the physiological impact of chronic stress because it can help balance cortisol and feeds the body and brain with balancing hormones and neurotransmitters. The endorphins produced by exercise—even those that come just from walking around the block—can provide a counter to the downward spiral of the stress response and reverse the emotional side-effects of acute and chronic stress. So exercise not only promotes your health, it also makes you more productive and able to focus on the task at hand.

The emotional benefits of exercise grow exponentially when they're combined with mindfulness practices. When exercise is meditative, it gives you an opportunity to create peace and get to know yourself again. By letting you take a step back from the physical and mental crunch of your busy life, mindful walking and breathing can bring you back to center while building your body and mind. As with any moving meditation this, too, can train you to maintain a thoughtful distance between yourself and each day's frustrations and obligations.

A BALANCED APPROACH TO FITNESS

Have you been turned off by today's notion of working out? If so, you're not alone. Many of us have an ambivalent relationship with working out—we don't exercise because we hate the gym, can't afford it, or don't have time to go there.

TOO MUCH EXERCISE

Believe it or not, you can actually exercise too much. This is of particular concern if you're already under a great deal of stress, because you'll raise your cortisol levels too high. Cortisol levels are higher for fitness-oriented people (particularly marathoners and tri-athletes) who don't take the time to recover between workouts or who pile high-output workouts onto high-stress days. Someone who runs 10 miles or cranks on the step machine for an hour and a half every night to blow off steam at the end of a long, stressful day could very well be exacerbating his stress hormone levels.

How do you know if you've reached that point? Athletes with elevated cortisol levels often become depressed; feel more tired than usual; experience colds, flu, or respiratory illness; and begin to suffer gastrointestinal symptoms. If you are experiencing some of these symptoms, back off of the hard-core exercise for a week or two, and just walk gently every day, instead. Be aware of why you exercise and how it makes you feel. It may be more beneficial to run 1 mile three times a week and walk or do yoga the other four days than it is to go full-throttle seven days a week. The body thrives on variety.

The good news, though, is that you don't need a gym in order to move your body. Besides, if you're in a crunch of noise, speed, crowds, and competition all day long as you're tethered to a computer or stuck in a car, the last thing you want is more of the same when you're tied to a machine or at a class at the gym. Daily sessions of knock-down-drag-out kickboxing and full-on, high-impact aerobics are not satisfying when life already seems like an obstacle course. You want a counterpoint to your challenges, not more of them.

Your goal is to balance your body chemistry and encourage a state of relaxation. To achieve this takes a balanced approach to fitness. For stress management, exercise should be moderate and consistent. The reason I try to emphasize continual and habitual movement over erratic, hour-long workouts is in part to keep cortisol at a low roar. But it's also easier to commit to two daily 20-minute at-home practices (one in the morning, one in the evening) than to a 1-hour workout at the gym. Again, morning and evening are the times of the day over which you have the most control, so routines made at these times are not easily foiled. Also, if movement is sustained throughout the day, so are its benefits. This is what we're after: consistent, strong, and supported body chemistry.

Choose fitness activities because you enjoy them, instead of picking what you think will give you the best body or burn the most calories. Focus on the idea of movement and breath—fitness will happen as a result. You'd be amazed at what a daily stroll can do for muscle tone, blood pressure, and mood. Walking is as powerful as it is undervalued. Taking a walk two or three times a week can lead to a significantly decreased risk of heart disease.

Of course, if going to the gym for aerobics works for you as both a release and a social outlet, by all means, go to the gym. Just make sure to maintain this program's bookends approach by using the 30-minute A.M. and P.M. windows for other stress-reducing activities such as an easy solitary walk, stretching, yoga, breathing exercises, or meditation. And remember, just because you go to the gym doesn't mean you shouldn't get up and move as often as possible every hour of the day.

MORNING FITNESS ROUTINE

An important part of an effective stress-management strategy is moving first thing in the morning. Exercising first thing is invigorating—so invigorating that you won't need to reach for caffeine and sugar to get you going. Beginning each day with an active, physical routine including stretching, cardiovascular and resistance training, and focused awareness on proper breathing engages endorphins and neurotransmitters, which are preventative buffers to stress hormones that may be activated during your day. This A.M. fitness routine, using a resistance cord, is designed to activate your mind and body and prepare you to meet all the challenges of the day, stress free.

A.M. FITNESS ROUTINE DIRECTIONS:

✳ Perform each exercise in the sequence shown, from start to finish.

✳ Follow the instructions presented and pay attention to yourself, your limits, and especially your breathing.

SEATED SPINE TWIST

When you first wake up in the morning, it's important to activate your upper body and spine to increase circulation and the flow of energy. Practice these simple stretching exercises to help jump-start your day.

FIG. 1

Sit in a chair with your feet hip-width apart. Be sure that you're seated in a position where your thighs and calves form as close to a 90-degree angle as possible. Grasp the handles of your resistance cord and raise your arms to shoulder height. Extend your arms out straight in front of you and pull the cord out to the sides, working and toning your arms and shoulders, and activating the circulation of blood and oxygen in your upper body. Breathe deeply, maintaining a long spine while keeping the cord stretched.

FIG. 2

Inhale deeply. On the exhalation, slowly turn your torso to the left. Initiate the turn from your hips and not your waist. Focus your vision on the center of the cord while maintaining outward pressure and resistance on the cord. On each exhalation, turn deeper into the twist. Continue this twist for 5 to 8 breaths, maintaining tension on the cord and deepening the stretch on each exhalation. Release the twist and repeat on the other side.

SEATED OVERHEAD SPINE STRETCH

The goal of this exercise is to reach up and out of your hips and spine, creating length in your waist to increase the energy flow through your upper body.

From the Seated Spine Twist, lower your arms back to shoulder height and grasp the resistance cord on the insides of the handles, palms facing outward. Apply outward tension on the cord. Inhale. On the exhalation, raise your arms straight overhead, reaching tall through your spine. Relax your shoulders while pressing firmly outward on the handles of the cord. Breathe.

Maintain the tension in the cord to stimulate and tone your arms as you take 5 to 8 long, deep breaths. Increase the lift through your spine on each exhalation.

MODIFIED SEATED FORWARD BEND

This exercise focuses on stretching your hamstrings to help create additional length in your lower spine, which helps maintain a healthy back. Perform this exercise anytime you feel tension building in your lower back, or anytime you simply need to unwind.

CLOSEUP DETAIL

From Seated Overhead Spine Stretch, release your arms down and fold forward from your waist, placing the resistance cord underneath your feet.

Grasp a handle in each hand, inhale, and on the exhalation, gently pull your torso downward, resting your chest on your thighs. Breathe deeply and comfortably. If your breath is irregular, back off the stretch slightly until you can maintain an even, comfortable breathing pattern. Keep tension on the cord to work and tone your arms while stretching your lower back, hips, and hamstrings. Hold for 5 to 8 deep breaths, maintaining tension on the cord and deepening the stretch through your hips and lower back on each exhalation.

STANDING FORWARD BEND

In this exercise you'll focus on stretching your hamstrings, which will afford you numerous physical benefits. You'll also benefit from the calming effects that forward bending can offer your body and mind. This exercise helps to calm your nervous system by slowing your heart rate and deeply stretching and rejuvenating your spine. Perform this exercise anytime you feel the need to unwind and calm yourself.

CLOSEUP DETAIL

Stand on top of your resistance cord with your feet together.

FIG. 1

Inhale and reach up tall through your spine. On the exhalation, slowly fold forward from your hips, keeping your knees slightly bent, and reach your hands to the floor, grasping the handles of your cord. Focus your vision ahead of you as you slowly begin to straighten your legs on each exhalation. Breathe deeply, concentrating on a long exhalation. Keep your shoulders relaxed and your neck soft, using the cord to help you stretch and lengthen your hamstrings. Do not force the stretch by pulling your torso down with the cord. Use your breath to deepen the stretch and the cord to support you.

FIG. 2

As your flexibility increases, work to increase the stretch by straightening your legs completely. Keep your shoulders and neck relaxed as you reach long through your spine, extending forward from your hips.

FIG. 3

Remove excess length in the cord by bringing your hands together and clasping both handles together. Maintain a comfortable breathing pattern and concentrate on lengthening through your spine and out of your hips. Don't force yourself forward, and keep your back straight at all times. Inhale and reach with your chest, exhale and lengthen your hamstrings up through your spine. Perform this exercise for 5 to 8 long, deep breaths, maintaining tension on the cord and deepening the stretch through your hips and lower back each time you exhale.

WIDE-LEG SEATED FORWARD BEND

This exercise promotes a deep opening of your hips and hamstrings, relieving tension in your lower back and sacrum. The wide-leg position helps stimulate your abdomen to relieve stress-related tension.

Start in a seated position with your legs extended out in front of you. Spread your legs as far apart as possible without leaning backward. Place your hands alongside your hips and press down, reaching up tall through your hips and spine. Inhale and lift your chest, then exhale and slowly lean forward from your hips, keeping your back straight and placing your hands on the floor in front of you. Hold the stretch at arms length, concentrating on extending up through your spine. Activate the muscles in your legs, reaching out firmly through your heels and pressing the backs of your knees to the floor. Breathe deeply and concentrate on keeping your back straight by reaching up through your spine and lifting your chest. As you get comfortable in the stretch, lean further forward. Keep your neck and shoulders relaxed. Hold this stretch for 5 to 8 long, even breaths.

Note: If you're a beginner or have less flexibility in your hips and hamstrings, start with your knees slightly bent and work up to stretching with straight legs.

RECLINED SINGLE-LEG TWIST

This exercise promotes a deep stretch in your lower back and waist. It's excellent for correcting an uneven posture and great for those who must work standing or sitting for long periods of time. This stretch is also a great way to maintain a healthy lower back and is a perfect stretch to perform throughout the day to alleviate lower-back tension.

Sit with your legs extended out in front of you. Slowly lower your torso to the floor, extending long through your spine and out through your heels. Bend your right leg and bring your right knee across your body to your left side at a 90-degree angle to your torso. Grasp your right knee with your left hand and extend your right arm out to the side at shoulder height, palm facing up. Focus your vision straight up above you. Inhale and lengthen through your spine and the bottom of your foot. Exhale, rotating your chest to the right and gently pushing your right knee to the floor. Keep your left leg extended and activated, reaching through the bottom of your foot. Allow your left leg to naturally rotate to the left as you deepen the stretch. Breathe deeply. Hold this stretch for 5 to 8 long, even breaths. Release and perform on the other side.

SEATED SINGLE-LEG TWIST

This exercise, which is similar to the Reclined Single-Leg Twist, promotes a deep stretch in your lower back, hips, and waist, and also helps expand your chest to stimulate your lungs for greater circulation and breathing capacity. This is a great stretch to perform after you've been standing for a long period of time.

From Reclined Single-Leg Twist, slowly press yourself up to a seated position with your legs extended out in front of you. Bend your right leg and cross your right foot over your left leg alongside your left knee. Slowly cross your right arm inside your right knee, and reach your hand down to the top of your right foot. Place your left hand back behind you to stabilize and support your torso. Position your hand so you can maintain an upright spine throughout the twisting motion. In this position, imagine a vertical line drawn from the top of your head straight down through your spine to the middle of your pelvis. This line is your reference point to initiate the twist.

Inhale. On the exhalation, slowly rotate your torso to the left, turning through the center line of your body, rotating your shoulders and opening your chest. Your vision should lead your rotation. Inhale and slightly release the twist, exhale and turn deeper into the twist. Keep your left leg active, pressing down through the back of your knee. Use your right arm to press against your right knee to help you open your torso and deepen the stretch. Maintain even and comfortable breathing. Hold this stretch for 5 to 8 long, even breaths. Release and perform on the other side.

SEATED CROSS-LEG TWIST

In this exercise you'll continue to focus on relieving tension and stress in your lower back, as you did with the Seated Single-Leg Twist. In addition to promoting a healthy spine, this exercise also helps alleviate stiffness in your ankles and knees while promoting a deeper stretch of your hips. It also encourages positive posture by focusing your mind on proper positioning to keep your spine erect.

Sit in a simple cross-legged posture. Make sure that you're sitting upright, squarely on your sit bones. To make this easier, reach under and pull the flesh of your buttocks back and away from your sit bones. Feel as if your pelvis is rolling forward in this position. Relax your hips and legs so that your knees will naturally fall open as far as they can. Inhale. On the exhalation, reach your left hand back behind you and your right hand across your lap, grasping your left knee. Hold and inhale. On the exhalation, gently pull with your right hand and reach back with your left hand. Use your left arm to stabilize and support your torso. Don't lean back—twist your torso through the center line of your body, rotating through your hips and shoulders. Open your chest and focus your vision behind you as you twist. Breathe. Each time you exhale, deepen the twist. Maintain even and comfortable breathing throughout the twisting motion. Hold this stretch for 5 to 8 long, even breaths. Release and perform the pose on the other side.

SEATED POWER ROWING

This exercise starts the resistance training portion of your morning routine. In Seated Power Rowing, you'll work your abdominals, lower back, and upper back. This combination promotes good posture and a healthy spine. It also tones your arms and stretches your legs so you have a full range of motion throughout your hip girdle.

CLOSEUP DETAIL

Sit on the floor with your legs extended out in front of you, feet and knees together. Bend your legs and wrap the resistance cord around the arches of your feet. Hold a handle of the cord in each hand and fully extend your legs out in front of you.

FIG. 1

Sit up tall through your spine and look straight ahead. Extend your arms straight out in front of you with your hands at navel height, just above your legs.

FIG. 2

Engage your abs and sit up tall—from your sit bones through your head—to support your lower back. Drop your shoulders down, engage your latissimus muscles (your outer back muscles, or lats), and pull with your hands back to your abdomen, below your chest. Hold, then release back to the starting position. Repeat. Exhale as you pull, inhale as you release.

Performance: Beginner—4 sets of 10 repetitions. Advanced—6 sets of 15 repetitions.

Positive Posture: During this exercise, you'll tend to lean back with the pull and forward with the release to gain leverage. To prevent this, sit up tall and engage your abdominals, and squeeze your buttocks muscles to support your torso.

CONCENTRATION ROWING

Similar to Seated Power Rowing, this exercise allows you to fully concentrate on the movement one arm at a time. Having to concentrate and focus intently on the movement and your breath can help you to better understand you body's language. Use concentration exercises to your full advantage and learn what your body is capable of.

CLOSEUP DETAIL

Start seated upright with your legs extended and 3 to 4 feet apart. Place the resistance cord around your right foot and grasp the cord with your left hand. Activate your feet, pressing through your heels, and keep your legs firm without locking your knees.

FIG. 1

Sit up tall through your spine and place your right hand directly behind you to lift and support your spine. Maintain a stable yet comfortable position that allows your shoulders to stay square and level with your waist and the floor. Engage your abs and fully extend your left arm toward your right foot.

FIG. 2

Keep your hand at navel height. Exhale and pull your left arm directly back alongside your ribcage. Hold and release. Repeat. Exhale as you pull, inhale as you release.

Performance: Beginners—4 sets of 10 repetitions on each side. Advanced—6 sets of 12 repetitions on each side.

Positive Posture: During this exercise, you'll tend to lean back and to the side with each pull to gain leverage. To prevent this, sit up tall and engage your abdominals to support your torso. Push firmly with your supporting hand, keeping your arm firm and stable. To gain better control of the movement, follow with your eyes as your arm extends and pulls back, contracting and releasing.

TORSO TONERS

This exercise helps tone and strengthen your entire upper body. The twisting motion with resistance helps to stabilize your abdomen and lower back—both key factors in supporting a healthy spine. In addition, the lateral movement helps to relieve built-up tension trapped in your spine.

CLOSEUP DETAIL

Sit upright with your legs extended and 3 to 4 feet apart. Place the resistance cord around your right foot and grasp the cord with both hands. Activate your feet, pressing through your heels, and keep your legs firm without locking your knees.

FIG. 1

Sit up tall through your spine, keeping your elbows slightly bent with your arms firm. Maintaining a locked, firm grip is key in this exercise because your arms act as a lever and are not involved directly in the action of the exercise. Keep your shoulders and waist level with the floor.

FIG. 2

Sit up tall through your spine and bring your hands to the center of your body, just above navel height. Inhale. On the exhalation, engage your abs and twist your torso to the left, leading with your chest and hands. Perform this twist all in one motion. When your hands go past your left leg, hold the position, then slowly release back to the center. Repeat. Exhale as you twist, inhale as you release.

Performance: Beginners—4 sets of 10 repetitions on each side. Advanced—6 sets of 12 repetitions on each side.

Positive Posture: During this exercise, you'll tend to lean to the side with each pull to gain leverage. To prevent this, sit up tall and firmly engage your abdominals to support your torso. Press firmly through your heels to help support your torso. To gain better control of the movement, follow with your eyes as your hands twist with your torso to each side.

BACK/ABS EXTENSIONS

This movement combines the benefits of several exercises into one. It strengthens your lower back while toning your abdominals—both of which are important to maintaining a healthy spine and well-balanced posture. And gripping the resistance cord, combined with the tension created in the movement, helps to tone your arms.

FIG. 1

Sit on the floor with your legs extended out in front of you, feet and knees together. Bend your legs and wrap the resistance cord around the arches of your feet. Hold a handle of the cord in each hand. Fully extend your legs. Sit up tall through your spine and lean slightly forward until there is minimal tension in the cord. Look straight ahead. Extend your arms straight out in front of you, keeping your hands at navel height.

FIG. 2

Press firmly through your feet, and activate your leg and buttocks muscles. Engage your abs and begin to slowly lean back, stretching the cord until you feel your abdominals fully engage, from bottom to top. Hold and breathe, using the cord for support. Count to 3 and draw yourself up, using your abs to bring you to a seated position. Repeat.

Performance: Beginners—Work up to 6 repetitions, holding for 3 to 5 counts. Advanced—Work up to 10 repetitions, holding for 5 to 8 counts.

Positive Posture: Pay attention to your body. Reach up tall through your spine throughout the exercise. Keep your neck relaxed, and look straight ahead. Maintain firm legs and reach through your feet. Only go back as far as is comfortable for you. You should be able to comfortably breathe while holding the contracted position.

MODIFIED COBRA—ABS AND BACK STRETCH

Including this exercise in your routine after performing abdominal or back exercises helps to effectively stretch both areas. This movement also helps tone your abs and is an excellent stretch for anyone who spends a lot of time standing or sitting.

Lie face down on your stomach, feet hip-width apart. Stretch your body out and reach long through the top of your head. Place your hands alongside your chest, fingers pointing forward. Inhale. On the exhalation, slowly press through your hands. Lift your chest off the floor and reach out through your head. Focus your vision straight ahead. Reach back and extend through your feet, keeping your legs active. Feel the stretch in your abs and feel your lower back releasing, allowing your body to reach and lift through your chest. Breathe. Hold for a count of 3, exhale, and release. Repeat.

Performance: Beginners—Work up to 6 repetitions, holding for 3 to 5 counts. Advanced—Work up to 10 repetitions, holding for 5 to 8 counts.

Positive Posture: Pay attention to your body. Keep your neck and shoulders relaxed and look straight ahead. Don't overextend and compress your lower back. Maintain active legs and stretch out long through your feet. Only raise your chest as far as is comfortable for you. You should be able to comfortably breathe while holding your chest in the raised position.

SEATED CONCENTRATION CURLS

This exercise tones and shapes your arms. In addition, curls also help keep your wrist and elbow joints strong, helping to prevent chronic aliments such as carpel tunnel syndrome.

CLOSEUP DETAIL

Position yourself on your sit bones squarely on the front edge of a chair. Separate your feet about hip-width apart and position your knees directly over your ankles. (This helps to stabilize and support a healthy posture.) Take your resistance cord and place it under your left foot. Hold the ends of the cord in your fingers, not your palms.

FIG. 1

Extend your arms straight down and sit up tall, keeping your spine erect and your shoulders square and level.

FIG. 2

Without lurching or jerking your body forward and back, slowly raise your left hand, focusing all your attention on the movement of your forearm and bicep. Pull upward until your forearm is parallel to the floor, hold, squeeze your bicep, and slowly release until your arm is fully extended. Repeat. Only your hand and forearm should move as you contract and re-lease the bicep muscle. Exhale as you pull, and inhale as you release. Keep the movement slow and simple. When you com-plete the repetitions with your left hand, repeat with your right.

Performance: Beginners—4 sets of 8 repetitions on each side. Advanced—6 sets of 15 repetitions on each side.

Positive Posture: You might tend to lean into the movement on the pull and fall away on the release. Keep your body firm by activating your abs. Press firmly through the balls and heels of your feet to maintain your foundation. Don't hunch your back.

SEATED OVERHAND CONCENTRATION CURLS

This movement is the flip side of the previous exercise, and it requires extra concentration and effort. It helps fully tone your arms, and the reverse grip aides in stabilizing your elbow and wrist joints, helping to prevent chronic tendonitis.

CLOSEUP DETAIL

As in Seated Concentration Curls, position yourself on your sit bones squarely on the front edge of a chair. Separate your feet about hip-width apart and position your knees directly over your ankles. Take your resistance cord and place it under your left foot. Hold the ends of the cord in the palms of your hands, not in your fingers.

FIG. 1

Extend your arms down, keeping your left elbow slightly bent. Sit up tall, keeping your spine erect and your shoulders square and level. Focus your attention straight ahead.

FIG. 2

Without lurching or jerking your body forward and back, slowly raise your left hand. Pull upward until your forearm is parallel to the floor, hold, and slowly release until your arm is fully extended. Repeat. Only your hand and forearm should move as you contract and release your bicep muscle. Exhale as you pull and inhale as you release. Keep the movement slow and simple. When you complete the required repetitions with your left hand, repeat with your right.

Performance: Beginners—4 sets of 8 repetitions on each side. Advanced—6 sets of 12 repetitions on each side.

Positive Posture: Because you might tend to lean into the movement, keep your body firm by activating your abs. Press firmly through the balls and heels of your feet to maintain your foundation. Don't hunch your back.

SEATED POWER CURLS

The principle behind power curls is to strengthen your arms while enhancing body coordination. The movement of this exercise is quicker than either form of concentration curls, but it requires as much focus to be performed properly. It's also a great exercise to elevate your heart rate, burn a few calories, and blow off some steam.

FIG. 1

Sit on the edge of your chair. Extend your left foot out in front of you and place your right foot firmly on the floor with your knee extend slightly beyond your foot for stability. Move your left foot out slightly wider than shoulder-width, extending through your heel. Make sure your torso is square with your hips and that your chest is pointing straight ahead. Place one handle of the resistance cord under the arch of your left foot and hold the other handle with your left hand. Extend your left arm straight down toward your left foot. Sit up tall, with your right arm extended down and gripping the chair directly behind your hip for stability.

FIG. 2

Without lurching or jerking your body forward and back, pull the cord firmly and quickly up toward your shoulder, curling and squeezing your bicep at the top of the movement. Pull as close to your shoulder as you can without moving your upper arm and elbow forward. Release quickly and smoothly, extending your arm completely. Focus all your attention on maintaining control during the movement. Exhale as you pull and inhale as you release.

Performance: Beginners—4 sets of 10 repetitions on each side. Advanced—6 sets of 15 repetitions on each side.

Positive Posture: Your upper arm might tend to move during the pull or release. To prevent this, keep your upper arm firm at your shoulder joint and watch your elbow. If it rises and falls with the movement, try to hold your upper arm in against your side. Keep your body firm by activating your abs.

TRICEP CURLS

This exercise isolates your upper arm by removing all leverage in the standing position. This movement helps strengthen your wrist and elbow joints and tone and enhance the shape of your arms. In addition, Tricep Curls focus on the area of the arm that is susceptible to being flabby.

FIG. 1

Face your chair. Bending your knees slightly, reach down and place your left hand on the seat of the chair. Spread your legs hip-width apart and stagger your foot placement so your right foot is forward, knee bent, and your left foot is back, reaching long and firm to create a strong foundation. Find a stable distance between your feet that is comfortable, yet stable and balanced, when you lean onto the chair. Make sure your feet remain firmly pressed into the floor at all times. Place the resistance cord under the arch of your right foot. Fully extend your left arm, keeping your hand flat on the chair directly under your shoulder joint. Keep your back flat, spine long, and focus your vision straight ahead. Position your right arm at a 90-degree angle, elbow tight to the side of your body, your hand slightly forward and pointing straight at your foot.

FIG. 2

Without leaning forward or down, slowly extend your right hand up and back toward your buttocks; keep your elbow tight to your body. Reach your hand back until your right arm is fully extended. Hold at the top, squeeze your tricep, and slowly release until your hand is pointing directly at your foot again. Repeat. Exhale as you reach back, inhale as you release forward. Keep the movement slow and simple. The entire movement in both directions should last the length of an exhalation and an inhalation.

Performance: Beginners—6 sets of 8 repetitions on each side. Advanced—8 sets of 12 repetitions on each side.

Positive Posture: You might tend to lean into the movement as you pull and press up as you release. Keep your body and support arm firm by pressing into the chair and using your arm as a brace for your torso. Press through the balls and heels of your feet to maintain your foundation. Don't hunch your back. Keep your abs strong for better support.

SEATED TRICEP FLIES

This exercise continues to work the backside of you upper arm (the tricep muscles). By performing this exercise sitting down, you eliminate active leverage from your body, which allows you to concentrate more effectively on the movement.

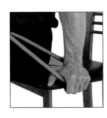

CLOSEUP DETAIL

Position yourself on your sit-bones squarely in the center of a chair. Separate your feet about hip-width apart and stack your knees directly over your ankles. This position helps stabilize and support a healthy posture. Take your resistance cord and place it under your left palm on the left edge of your chair. Use your hand to press down on the handle, pinning the cord to the chair.

FIG. 1

Cross the other handle of the cord over your lap, grasping the cord in the fingers of your right hand, not in your palm. Bend your right arm at approximately a 45-degree angle and raise your right hand up to navel height with your elbow pointing out to the side. This is your starting position. Press your right arm down and sit up tall, keeping your spine erect and shoulders square and level.

FIG. 2

Inhale deeply. As you exhale, reach your right hand up and out at a 45-degree angle, extending your arm from the elbow upward to just above shoulder height. Hold, then release back down to the starting position. As soon as your hand comes to the starting point, reach back up and extend your hand outward from the elbow, as before. Hold, squeeze your tricep at the top, and release. Breathe with the movement; exhale as you reach upward, inhale as you release back to your starting position. Keep the movement quick and controlled.

Performance: Beginners—6 sets of 10 repetitions on each side. Advanced—8 sets of 15 repetitions on each side.

Positive Posture: During this exercise you'll feel a slight up and down motion in your torso. This is natural due to the motion of the exercise itself. To work the core of your body, keep your back long and work to stabilize your core with your abs. Keep your left arm pressing firmly into the chair. Press through the balls and heels of your feet to maintain your foundation. Don't hunch your back.

SEATED ANTERIOR DELTOID FLIES

You'll now move on to working your shoulders. You'll start with the front deltoids—the small muscle group that helps you raise your arms up when you drink a glass of water. This next set of three exercises helps to strengthen your shoulder joints and enhance shoulder mobility by strengthening smaller muscles that may be inactive.

FIG. 1

Position yourself on your sit bones, squarely on the front edge of a chair. Separate your feet about hip-width apart and stack your knees directly over your ankles. Take your resistance cord and place it under the arch of your right foot. Hold the opposite end of the cord in the palm of your right hand. Grip the edge of the chair alongside your left hip with your left hand. Press down firmly with your left hand to stabilize your body during the exercise. Extend your right arm straight out, directly above your right knee, keeping your spine erect and shoulders square and level. Keep your right elbow facing out to your side and the palm of your right hand facing down at all times. (This means to rotate your arm to the outside. You will feel this when you begin the movement.) Work to keep your elbow rotated outward, and focus all resistance on your shoulder. Press firmly through your feet, keep your legs strong, and engage your buttocks and abs.

FIG. 2

Inhale. As you exhale, engage your abs and raise your right hand straight up to shoulder height, hold, and release back down to your knee. Repeat. The movement should be even and smooth. Count up 2, hold, and count down 2. Exhale as you lift, inhale as you release.

Performance: Beginners—4 sets of 8 repetitions on each side. Advanced—6 sets of 12 repetitions on each side.

Positive Posture: During this exercise, you may tend to lean forward and back. To prevent this, spread your feet slightly until you have strengthened the core of your body and found your balance. Engage your buttocks and abdominal muscles for control.

SEATED MEDIAL DELTOID FLIES

This exercise works the outsides of your shoulders. The medial deltoid is the muscle that allows you to lift your arms out to your sides. If you want to build wider, more athletic-looking shoulders, this is the exercise for you.

CLOSEUP DETAIL

Position yourself on your sit-bones, squarely on the front edge of a chair. Separate your feet about hip-width apart and stagger your feet so your right foot is in front of your left, feet firmly planted on the floor. Take your resistance cord and place it under the arch of your left foot. Hold the opposite handle of the cord in the palm of your right hand with the cord extended across and under your right leg.

FIG. 1

Grip the edge of the chair alongside your left hip with your left hand. Press down firmly with your left hand to stabilize your body during the exercise. Extend your right arm straight down alongside your right hip, keeping your spine erect, shoulders square and level. Keep your right elbow rotated out and facing backward, and keep the palm of your right hand facing down at all times. Work to keep your elbow rotated back, and focus all the resistance on the outside of your shoulder. Press firmly through your feet, keep your legs strong, and engage your buttocks and abs.

FIG. 2

Inhale. As you exhale, engage your abs and raise your right hand straight out to the side, as high as you can without forcing the movement. Hold, and release back down. Repeat. The movement should be even and smooth. Count up for 2, hold, and count down for 2. Exhale as you lift and inhale as you release. Keep the elbow of your right arm firm, but not locked.

Performance: Beginners—4 sets of 8 repetitions on each side. Advanced—6 sets of 12 repetitions on each side.

Positive Posture: During this exercise, you might tend to lean away from the movement to gain leverage. To prevent this, spread your feet slightly until you have strengthened the core of your body and found your balance. Remember to engage your buttocks and abdominal muscles for control.

SEATED POSTERIOR DELTOID FLIES

This exercise helps to strengthen the rear of your shoulder girdle, which helps prevent you from slouching if you've been standing or sitting for a long period of time.

CLOSEUP DETAIL

Position yourself on your sit-bones, squarely on the front edge of a chair. Separate your feet about hip width-apart and stack your knees directly over your ankles. This position helps to stabilize and support a healthy posture. Take your resistance cord and place it in the palm of your left hand. Now place your left hand up against the left side of your body, just above your hip.

FIG. 1

Hold the opposite end of the cord in the palm of your right hand, and extend your right arm straight out in front of you at shoulder height, keeping your spine erect and your shoulders square and level. Keep your right elbow facing out to the side and the palm of your right hand facing toward the center of your body at all times. You will feel the extra resistance when you begin the movement. Work to keep your elbow rotated outward, and focus all resistance on your shoulder. Press firmly through your feet, keep your legs strong, and engage your buttocks and abs.

FIG. 2

Press your feet firmly into the floor and engage your legs, buttocks, and abs. Inhale. As you exhale, swing your right hand out to the side, in line with your torso. Imagine you're opening a door. Keep your arm straight and your elbow firm, but not locked. Your elbow joint should point out to the side and away from you throughout the movement. Your palm should face into the centerline of your body. Repeat. The movement should be even and smooth. Count to 2 as you extend, hold, and count to 2 as you release. Exhale as you extend, inhale as you release.

Performance: Beginners—4 sets of 8 repetitions on each side. Advanced—6 sets of 12 repetitions on each side.

Positive Posture: During this exercise, you'll tend to lean away from or into the movement to gain leverage. To prevent this, spread your feet slightly until you have strengthened the core of your body and found your balance. Engage your buttocks and abdominal muscles for control. Look straight ahead and find a focus point—it will help you find balance and prevent leaning.

EVENING YOGA PRACTICE

Taking time at the end of the day to unwind, relax, and destress will help promote a more restful, healing sleep and allow you to be more prepared for the next day. The following invigorating and restorative yoga practice can help you bring each day to a close feeling calm. It combines powerful yoga postures with deep breathing that will release tension from your muscles, oxygenate your system, and focus your mind. Practice this sequence each evening and you'll begin to experience a more relaxed, stress-free body and a more focused, centered mind.

P.M. YOGA PRACTICE DIRECTIONS:

* Perform each posture in the sequence as shown, from start to finish.

* If time is short or you're looking to reap the benefits of a specific pose, hold the pose for up to 1 minute with attention to comfortable, relaxed breathing.

P.M.

MOUNTAIN POSE

Mountain Pose is the starting place for all standing yoga poses. Done correctly, this upright, firm posture reduces stress and can increase your focus.

FIG. 1

Stand tall with your feet together, heels and big toes touching. Spread your toes out. Extend your arms down at your sides, fingers pointing toward the floor. Reach up tall through your head, looking straight ahead. Breathe deeply and consistently.

FIG. 2

To feel the posture and find the proper position, be firm with your legs. Tighten your knees slightly and firm your buttocks. Keeping your stomach strong, lift your chest, spine, and neck straight up, as if a rope was pulling you skyward through the center of your body. Breathe. Hold this posture for 5 long, even breaths, working up to holding the pose for a full minute.

Note: Balance your weight evenly between your heels and your toes.

Option: If you're a beginner, you can start with your feet spread apart slightly and your heels and back pressed firmly against a wall.

MOUNTAIN POSE WITH ARMS OVERHEAD

Mountain Pose with Arms Overhead is a great pose for anyone who spends too much time sitting down. This posture helps exercise the joints of the shoulders, arms, and wrists.

To complete Mountain Pose, inhale, and then exhale while raising your arms overhead, hands shoulder-width apart, fingers reaching skyward. Drop your shoulders down your back. Reach as tall as you can. Breathe. Hold this posture for 5 long, even breaths, working up to holding the pose for a full minute.

Note: Don't scrunch your shoulders to reach. Relax your neck, feeling your shoulders fall back and down.

Option: If you're a beginner, try this pose against the wall to start.

STANDING FORWARD BEND

This posture allows your spine to stretch deeply and lengthens your hamstrings, which gives you numerous physical benefits. However, the purpose of this exercise in this context is the calming effects that forward bending can offer your body and mind. This posture helps calm your nervous system by slowing your heart rate and rejuvenating your spinal column. Perform this posture anytime you feel the need to unwind and calm yourself.

FIG. 1

From Mountain Pose with Arms Overhead, bend your knees slightly, inhale, and as you exhale bend forward with knees bent, placing your hands on the floor alongside your toes. Keep your back straight and long, and keep your neck soft.

FIG. 2

Keeping your legs strong, extend out through your waist and allow your upper body to fold forward, straightening your legs. Breathe. This posture is meant to be relaxing and calming; forcing the pose negates its benefits. You should be able to breathe evenly and comfortably in this posture. Hold this posture for 5 long, even breaths, working up to holding the pose for a full minute.

FIG. 3

If you can't touch the floor, use a yoga brick as an extension of your arms. This will allow you to extend your legs straight without bowing at your waist. If you don't have a yoga brick, use a big, firm book or a stack of books. (You want about 9 inches of height.)

FIG. 4

If you're fairly flexible, move into the complete posture by fully extending your legs and wrapping your hands behind your ankles. Reach long through your spine and waist, bringing your head to your knees.

PUSH-UP POSE

You'll have to concentrate to perform this posture correctly. When done properly, Push-Up Pose can help relieve lethargy in the body.

FIG. 1

In Standing Forward Bend, inhale. As you exhale, reach your hands to the floor and step your feet back behind you, lowering yourself to push-up position about 6 inches above the floor. Breathe. Keep your elbows tight to your body and your stomach strong and firm. Balance your weight evenly between your hands and toes. Breathe. Maintain a long, firm body as you gaze down slightly in front of you. Breathe. Hold this posture for 5 long, even breaths, working up to holding the pose for a full minute.

Note: Your hands should be directly alongside your chest, fingers below your armpits.

FIG. 2

If you have less arm strength, relax your knees down to the floor, keeping your arms strong. Your buttocks will elevate slightly, so focus on balancing the weight of your body evenly between your hands, knees, and feet. Breathe.

UPWARD FACING DOG

This posture is best known for stretching, strengthening, and rejuvenating the spine. It also helps to expand your chest and lungs, giving you more cardiovascular capacity, which allows you to breathe more deeply to help relieve stress.

In Push-Up Pose, inhale. As you exhale, release your entire body to the floor. Move your hands alongside your waist, keeping your elbows tight to the sides of your body. Turn your toes back. Gaze forward. Breathe.

Spread your feet about hip-width apart. Inhale. As you exhale, pull your trunk forward and raise your head upward, pressing firmly with your hands and fully extending your arms. Breathe. Keep your legs firm and strong, your knees lifted off the floor. Push your chest forward and up, completely stretching your spine and thighs. Reach tall through your arms and keep your buttocks tight. Relax your shoulders down your back and away from your ears, creating space for additional length in the pose. Breathe deeply and evenly. Hold this posture for 5 long, even breaths, working up to holding the pose for a full minute.

To release the pose, bend your elbows and release your torso to the floor.

DOWNWARD FACING DOG

The most beneficial pose in the yoga repertoire, this posture helps relieve fatigue, exhaustion, and headaches. It stimulates blood flow to the head and chest, which rejuvenates brain cells and slows your heart rate. This pose is invigorating and calming, all in one action. It also helps tone your legs, arms, and abdomen.

FIG. 1

Lying flat on the floor, keep your feet about hip-width apart. Position your hands alongside your chest. Inhale. As you exhale, press your palms into the floor and raise your torso up, straightening your arms. Drop your head toward your feet while pushing back, straightening your elbows, and extending your back. Raise your hips to the sky as you press through your legs and extend back from your arms through your shoulders. Bend your knees slightly, and begin to press back through your heels. Breathe. Relax your neck and release your shoulders back. Feel as though your shoulder blades want to touch in the middle of your back. Keep your feet and hands pointing straight ahead. Hold this posture for 5 long, even breaths, working up to holding the pose for a full minute.

FIG. 2

Once your feel comfortable or you have more flexibility, begin to straighten your knees and press firmly back through your heels. Remember to relax your shoulders. Breathe. To release the pose, inhale, and as you exhale, bend your knees and drop your hips toward the floor. Step forward with your right foot, keeping your left foot in place. Raise your torso straight up for Warrior I.

WARRIOR I

The posture helps strengthen your legs, ankles, and spine, and creates flexibility in your knee joints. It also helps expand your chest for deeper breathing and tone your abdomen for better digestion.

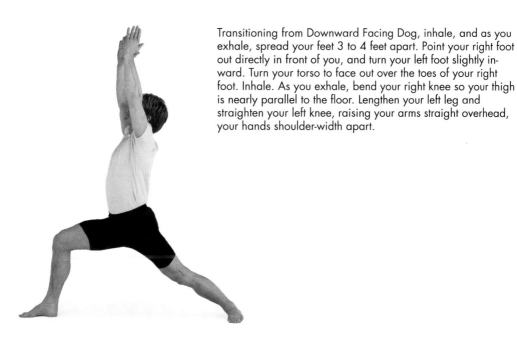

Transitioning from Downward Facing Dog, inhale, and as you exhale, spread your feet 3 to 4 feet apart. Point your right foot out directly in front of you, and turn your left foot slightly inward. Turn your torso to face out over the toes of your right foot. Inhale. As you exhale, bend your right knee so your thigh is nearly parallel to the floor. Lengthen your left leg and straighten your left knee, raising your arms straight overhead, your hands shoulder-width apart.

OVERVIEW

Your right knee, hips, chest, and head should be facing directly out over your right foot. Breathe. Stretch your arms tall overhead; relax your shoulders down your back, keeping your neck soft. Focus your vision straight ahead of you. Press firmly through both feet. Breathe. Hold this posture for 5 long, even breaths. Come slowly up to a standing position and bring your arms down by your sides. Perform the pose on the opposite side, with your left leg forward and your right leg back, holding for 5 long, even breaths. Work up to holding the pose for a full minute on each side.

WARRIOR II

A continuation of Warrior I, this posture helps to increase flexibility in your hips and knees. It also develops strength and endurance in your legs. It vigorously tones your entire torso and helps increase your breathing capacity.

From Warrior I, straighten your left leg, lower your arms to shoulder height, turn your right foot out 90 degrees, and turn your left foot in slightly. Reach long through your fingers and turn your head to face out toward your right hand. Inhale. As you exhale, bend your right knee so your thigh is nearly parallel to the floor. Lengthen your left leg and straighten your left knee. Try to create a 90-degree angle between your thigh and calf. Breathe.

OVERVIEW

Stretch your back leg firmly. Extend out through your hands, keeping your hips in line with your chest. Breathe. Your right knee should be facing directly out over your right foot. Stretch your arms wide and keep your hands at shoulder height. Relax your shoulders down your back, keeping your neck soft. Focus your vision out and over your right hand. Press firmly through both feet, reaching long through your back leg. Breathe. Hold this posture for 5 long, even breaths and then move to the other side, moving your left leg forward and your right leg back. Work up to holding the pose for a full minute on each side.

TRIANGLE

This lateral posture helps deeply stretch and open your body while strengthening and toning your legs, hips, back, and arms. It also helps to correct postural imbalances while it expands your chest and stimulates your digestive system.

FIG. 1

From Warrior II, straighten your left leg, keeping your arms at shoulder height. Turn your right foot out to 90 degrees and your left foot in slightly. Inhale. As you exhale, reach long through your spine and slowly reach your right hand down to your right ankle. Rotate your chest and left hip open. Reach your left arm straight up to the sky, turning your head up and gazing at your left hand. Maintain a strong base through both feet, and breathe. On each exhalation, work to open your chest and hips, reaching tall through your left hand. Keep your neck and shoulders relaxed. Breathe.

OVERVIEW

Alignment is key in this posture. Be sure that your feet and heels are positioned directly in line with one another. Work to achieve full rotation through your chest and hips, creating a flat posture while reaching tall through your raised hand. As your flexibility improves, move your bottom hand to the floor on the outside of your forward foot. Hold this posture for 5 long, even breaths and then move to the other side, keeping your left leg forward and your right leg back. Work up to holding the pose for a full minute on each side.

FIG. 2

If you have less flexibility in your hips and legs, place a yoga brick on the floor next to your forward foot, to help you with the extension.

EXTENDED SIDE ANGLE POSE

The long extension of this posture deeply stretches the entire side of your body, strengthens and stabilizes your legs, and helps to tone your waist. In addition, the extended angle of the pose helps improve lung capacity by opening up your chest.

FIG. 1

From Triangle, switch your stance by turning your right foot out 90 degrees and your left foot in slightly. Inhale. As you exhale, bend your right knee to a 90-degree angle and reach your right hand down to the floor outside your right foot. Inhale again. As you exhale, raise your left hand straight up to the sky, rotating your chest and hips open. Breathe. Keep your legs strong and press firmly through your feet, keeping your neck and shoulders relaxed. Focus your vision up toward your raised hand. With each exhalation, work to open your chest and hips further. Breathe evenly and comfortably. Hold this posture for 5 long, even breaths and then move to the other side, left leg forward and right leg back. Work up to holding the pose for a full minute on each side.

FIG. 2

If you're not very flexible through your hips and legs, place a yoga brick on the floor next to your forward foot for added extension.

STANDING WIDE-LEG FORWARD BEND

The wide extension of the legs in this posture helps tone your thighs and calves while creating flexibility in your hamstrings and lower back. The forward bend increases blood flow to your upper body and head, invigorating your spine and nervous system.

FIG. 1

From Extended Side Angle Pose, straighten your left leg and raise your torso to a standing position. Keeping your legs wide, turn your feet forward so they are parallel and place your hands on your hips. Reach tall through your spine and breathe deeply. As you exhale, fold forward from your hips and reach your hands down to the floor in front of you, directly below your shoulders. Keep your legs strong and press firmly through your feet. Keep reaching long through your spine and up through your hips, with a relaxed neck and shoulders. Hold this posture for 5 long, even breaths, working up to holding the pose for a full minute.

FIG. 2

If you aren't very flexible through your hips and legs, place a yoga brick on the floor for added extension.

STANDING FORWARD BEND

This posture helps calm your nervous system by slowing your heart rate and rejuvenating your spinal column. Perform this posture anytime you feel the need to unwind and calm yourself.

FIG. 1

From Standing Wide-Leg Forward Bend, bend your knees slightly and inhale. Exhale, raising your torso up and walking your feet together to Mountain Pose. Inhale. As you exhale, bend your knees slightly and bend forward, placing your hands on the floor alongside your toes. (If you're a beginner, you can place your hands in front of your toes.) Keep your back straight and your neck long and soft.

FIG. 2

Keeping your legs strong, extend out through your waist and allow your upper body to fold forward, straightening your legs. Breathe. This posture is meant to be relaxing and calming; forcing the pose negates its benefits. You should be able to breathe evenly and comfortably in this posture. Hold for 5 long, even breaths, working up to holding the pose for a full minute.

Option: If you have more flexibility, move into the complete posture by fully extending your legs and wrapping your hands behind your ankles. Reach long through your spine and waist, bringing your head to your knees.

CHILD'S POSE

This is a restorative posture that allows you to relieve pressure on your lower back and realign your spine. Resting your forehead on your forearms helps to relieve tension in your head. This posture is also beneficial in developing proper abdominal breathing.

From Standing Forward Bend, bend your knees and lower yourself to the floor in a kneeling position. Rest your buttocks on your heels and sit up tall. Inhale. As you exhale, slowly drop your torso forward. Rest your chest and abdomen on your thighs. Fold your arms in front of you and rest your forehead on your forearms. Allow your entire upper body to rest comfortably. Let your legs relax and spread open slightly, if necessary. You should feel the weight of your body resting on your thighs and tension releasing from your back. Take 5 long, even breaths, working up to holding the pose for a full minute.

HERO'S POSE

This posture is recommended if you stand or sit for long periods of time during the day. This pose helps relieve stiffness in your hips and knees, reduces inflammation in your legs from standing for long periods of time, and alleviates pain in your feet, ankles, and calves. It also helps increase blood circulation throughout your body.

FIG. 1

From Child's Pose, slowly press yourself up to a kneeling position. Bring your knees to hip-width apart, with your buttocks resting comfortably between your feet and ankles. Try to rest your buttocks to the floor. Inhale. As you exhale, interlace your fingers, turn your palms inside out, and raise your arms straight overhead.

FIG. 2

Relax your legs and hips and reach long through your spine. On each exhalation, concentrate on releasing your shoulder blades down and away from your neck, keeping your neck soft. Reach tall through your arms, keeping your torso balanced evenly over your hips and waist. Don't lean forward or backward. Breathe. Hold this posture for 5 long, even breaths, working up to holding the pose for a full minute.

FIG. 3

If you're not very flexible in your legs and hips, use a Baby Bolster or blanket to raise your hips off the floor, creating the necessary space to comfortably sit in the position.

HERO'S POSE WITH SPINE TWIST

Here you'll increase the benefits of Hero's Pose by adding a twisting motion. The twist helps to relieve pressure in your lower back and tension in your abdomen, aiding in overall body circulation and digestion. This posture also helps to expand your chest and condition your lungs to increase your breathing capacity.

FIG. 1

From Hero's Pose, release your arms down to the floor alongside your hips. Inhale deeply. As you exhale, slowly twist your upper body to the left. Place your left hand on the floor behind your left hip. Place your right hand on your left thigh, just above your knee. On each exhalation, increase the twist and concentrate on lifting through your spine, turning your shoulders and spine from the waist. Turn your head into the twist as you exhale. Hold and twist with each exhalation for 3 to 5 deep breaths. Release slowly and repeat on the other side.

FIG. 2

If you don't have much flexibility through your shoulders, spine, and hips, place a yoga brick directly behind your hip for added height and support.

STAFF POSE

This pose is the starting place of all seated forward postures, which is the beginning of the end of our sequence. Consistently practicing this pose—particularly if you sit for long periods of time during the day—will help to correct your posture, alleviate tension in your spine and legs, and stimulate your abdomen and pelvic regions for better circulation.

FIG. 1

From Hero's Pose with Spine Twist, extend your legs out in front of you with your feet side by side and touching each other. Position yourself by pulling the flesh of your buttocks back so that you are seated on your sit-bones. Place both hands on the floor directly alongside your hips, fingers pointing forward. Relax and release your shoulder blades down away from your ears and reach tall through your spine. Relax the tension in your abdomen and breathe deeply, taking long, relaxed breaths. Press through your hands to lift your spine. Keep your shoulders and abdomen relaxed. Extend long through your heels and activate your legs to create length through your hamstrings. Breathe. Hold this posture for 5 long, even breaths, working up to holding the pose for a full minute.

FIG. 2

If you're a beginner or you're not very flexible in your hips and waist, perform this posture sitting on a yoga brick positioned directly under your sit-bones.

OVERVIEW

Find balance in your posture. Lift straight up, don't lean to one side or the other, and press firmly through your hands for support. Reaching long through your heels will help you stabilize your posture. Be sure to keep your shoulders and waist level. Don't lean forward or backward.

SEATED FORWARD BEND

This pose helps calm your nervous system and alleviates stress and tension in both your body and mind. The posture stretches the entire back of your body, from your feet to your head. It also helps develop flexibility in your legs, which helps to support your lower back.

FIG. 1

From Staff Pose, inhale deeply. As you exhale, reach tall through your spine and bend forward from your waist, reaching your hands to your feet. Relax your neck and shoulders and lift through your chest. Breathe deeply and comfortably. On each exhalation, relax deeper into the stretch, bending even further forward and bringing your chest toward your thighs. Hold this posture for 5 long, even breaths, working up to holding the pose for a full minute.

FIG. 2

If you're a beginner or you have less flexibility in your hamstrings, use a yoga strap to extend your arms so you can comfortably bend forward from your hips. If you find that you're reaching with your head (creating a curve in your back), release the pose and use a strap until you gain more flexibility in your legs and hips. Beginners can also use a yoga brick under their sit-bones for added height in the hips so they can perform the pose more comfortably.

SINGLE-LEG SEATED FORWARD BEND

A simple derivative of the Seated Forward Bend, this posture helps you to concentrate more deeply on each leg individually in the forward bend position, helping to intensify the stretch and creating more flexibility in your hamstrings, hips, and spine.

FIG. 1

From Seated Forward Bend, tuck your left foot and heel into your groin with your knee bent outward at about a 90-degree angle. Reach long through your right heel and activate your right leg by pressing down through your knee. Extend tall through your spine, relaxing your neck and shoulders and keeping your back as straight as possible. Inhale deeply. As you exhale, lift up through your hips and reach your hands to your right foot, folding forward from your waist. Breathe. Position your torso directly over your extended leg, bringing your head toward your extended knee. With each exhalation, extend deeper into the stretch and bring your chest closer to your thigh. Hold this posture for 5 long, even breaths and then move to the other side. Work up to holding the pose for a full minute on each side.

FIG. 2

If you're a beginner or you have less flexibility in your hamstrings, use a yoga strap to extend your arms so you can comfortably bend forward from your hips. Or if you find that you're reaching with your head (creating a curve in your back), release the pose and use a strap until you gain more flexibility in your legs and hips. Beginners can also use a yoga brick under their sit-bones for added height in their hips so they can perform the pose more comfortably.

WIDE-LEG SEATED FORWARD BEND

This posture promotes a deep opening of your hips and hamstrings, relieving tension in your lower back and sacrum. This wide-leg position helps stimulate the abdomen to relieve stress-related tension. It's also a great pose for women who suffer from painful menstrual periods.

FIG. 1

Start in a seated position with your legs extended out in front of you. Spread your legs as far apart as possible without losing your balance on your sit-bones or leaning backward. Pull the flesh of your buttocks back so that you are comfortably seated on your sit-bones. Place your hands alongside your hips and press down, reaching your torso up tall from your hips and through your spine. Breathe. Inhale and lift your chest; as you exhale, slowly lean forward, keeping your back straight and placing your hands on the floor directly in front of you. Hold the pose, concentrating on extending up through your spine. Activate your legs, reaching out firmly through your heels and pressing the backs of your knees to the floor. Breathe deeply and concentrate on keeping your back straight by reaching up through your spine and lifting your chest. Breathe into your groin to release tension. As you get comfortable in the pose, begin to lean further forward until you feel a release in your hips and hamstrings. Keep your neck and shoulders relaxed. Hold this posture for 5 long, even breaths, working up to holding the pose for a full minute.

FIG. 2

If you're a beginner or you have less flexibility in your hips and hamstrings, place a yoga brick directly under your sit-bones to give added height to your hips, which will help you perform the pose more comfortably.

BUTTERFLY POSE

Butterfly Pose concentrates on stretching your inner thighs and groin to stimulate blood flow to that area. This helps promote a healthy pelvis, abdomen, and lower back. This pose also helps stretch your hips and thighs to relieve stress-related tension caused by sitting for long periods of time. Butterfly Pose helps relieve menstrual pain.

FIG. 1

From Wide-Leg Seated Forward Bend, release your legs, drawing each heel into your groin and releasing your knees out to the sides. Place the bottoms of your feet flat against each other. Hold your feet and slowly draw your heels deeper into your groin area. Lift up tall from your hips through your spine and chest. Keep your back straight while you continue to draw your heels into your groin. Once you have found a comfortable position, place your hands directly behind your buttocks and hips. Press through your palms, lifting your spine and chest upward. Relax your hips and allow your knees to drop further toward the floor. Breathe deeply and comfortably. Hold this posture for 5 long, even breaths, working up to holding the pose for a full minute.

FIG. 2

If you're a beginner or have less flexibility in your hips, place a yoga brick under your sit-bones to give added height to your hips, and keep your hands on your ankles, drawing your heels into your groin, which will help you perform the pose more comfortably.

RECLINED COBBLER POSE

This posture is known as the restorative version of Butterfly Pose. In the reclined position you'll continue to deeply stretch your thighs and hips to stimulate circulation in your pelvis, abdomen, and lower back. This helps relieve stress-related tension in your abdomen and lower back, sciatica, and stress-related indigestion. It also helps alleviate menstrual pain.

From Butterfly Pose, use your arms to slowly release your torso down to the floor. Keep your feet together and knees wide. Relax your neck and release your shoulder blades down and away from your ears. Place your hands on your belly and relax your hips, releasing your knees down toward the floor. Breathe. Concentrate on letting go of all sensations and allow your body to melt into the floor. Feel the rise and fall of your abdomen as you breathe deeply. Hold this posture for up to 3 minutes with attention to comfortable, relaxed breathing.

SUPPORTED CORPSE POSE

In this variation of the classic relaxation posture Corpse Pose, you'll use a bolster to elevate your chest and diaphragm, which increases your breathing capacity and stimulates the flow of oxygen to your body. This posture is not meant to be meditative; it's a pose to stimulate energy flow throughout your body to help reduce stress.

From Reclined Cobbler Pose, release and extend your legs out in front of you. Slowly roll onto your right side. Using your arms, press yourself up to a seated position and place the end of a bolster against your lower back and hips. Slowly release yourself back down onto the bolster with your spine and head resting on the top. You should feel a lift through your chest and a stretch through your abdomen. Your hips and waist should be raised slightly off the floor. Allow your shoulders to open out to the sides and your arms to rest comfortably out and away from your body, palms facing upward. Open your feet about shoulder-width apart and let your legs naturally fall open from your hips. Let your entire body sink into the floor and bolster. Breathe deeply and comfortably, concentrating on relaxing your body from head to toe and breathing deeply into your chest. Hold this posture for up to 3 minutes with attention to comfortable, relaxed breathing.

CORPSE POSE

In this pose, you'll try to remain motionless. Practicing the art of remaining motionless will help you keep your mind still, bringing you into a state of conscious relaxation, which helps to relieve stress and tension. The practice of conscious relaxation invigorates your body and refreshes your mind.

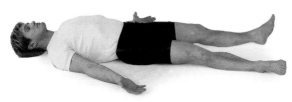

From Supported Corpse Pose, slowly roll onto your right side and take few long, deep breaths to awaken your mind. Using your arms, press yourself up to a seated position, keeping your legs extended out in front of you. Remove the bolster and slowly release yourself back down to the floor. Position your feet just wider than shoulder-width apart, allowing your legs to naturally fall open from your hips. Relax your neck and release your shoulders down and away from your ears. Let your arms rest slightly out and away from your sides, palms facing upward. Breathe deeply and evenly; close your eyes and feel your body sink into the floor. Stay in this pose for up to 15 minutes. Concentrate on deep breaths with long exhalations.

To come out of the pose, slowly roll onto your right side and take a few long, deep breaths to awaken your mind. Using your arms, press yourself up to a seated position and cross your legs in front of you for a few moments, resting in a simple cross-legged position.

6

Revamping Your Diet

How well do you eat?

Diet plays as major a role in stress management as exercise does. That's because a poor diet can actually cause an unhealthy response to stress. What you eat, as well as when and how you eat, can create chemical changes in your body that produce internal stress and, at the same time, weaken your capacity to deal with external stress. Unfortunately, what many people consider to be normal habits are in fact quite detrimental to their health. Do you think it's okay to have a catch-as-catch-can approach to food, grabbing snacks when you're about to drop from hunger instead of having meals at consistent times? Do you think it's no big deal if you don't have time for breakfast or you forget to eat lunch? The fact is, eating poorly is a big deal. Skipping meals creates unstable blood sugar levels, challenges insulin, and impairs metabolism, all of which sap your body's energy. On the other hand, overeating overworks your digestive system—and if what you're eating also happens to be a high-sugar, low-nutrient snack, your blood sugar levels take another hit. Doing both—skipping meals and then overeating to compensate (which is common)—is nothing short of a knock-down-drag-out loss for your whole system.

In addition, the more stressed you are, the more your body becomes depleted of key nutrients, vitamins, and amino acids that support optimal neurotransmitter levels, as well as aid the body's adrenal system.

GETTING A GRIP ON BLOOD SUGAR

Not only do we lose nutrients during chronic stress, but we also don't choose the foods that will replenish their stores. Chronic stress can erode your optimal levels of key neurotransmitters. In particular, chronic stress combined with unbalanced and nonnutrient dense foods can challenge your stores of serotonin and subsequently lead to a craving for simple sugary carbohydrates. It's a nonnegotiable response. How often during a really long and stressful day do you say, "Give me some broccoli. Let me at that bok choy!" It's rare. There's a chemical reason you go for chocolate, breads, and baked goods at that 4 P.M. slump and reach for wine or beer at the end of a long day.

But by reaching for simple sugars—foods that are the least nutrient-dense—we invite inflammation into the body, and we make ourselves candidates for a blood sugar heyday. Once those glucose levels become unstable, it becomes difficult to set them straight. As much as you might want to make the right choice, you can't. Your chemistry wins under unmitigated stress.

Of course, what goes up must come down. When glucose spikes in the body, its levels later crash. The brain responds to this drastic drop in its primary food source as a potential starvation situation, setting off alarms calling for more glucose. As you know, when stuck in a state of stress, the body dumps sugar and fatty acids into the blood to prepare it for action. Even without eating simple carbohydrates, blood sugar levels are challenged. Feeding an existing chemical roller coaster with sweets is the last thing you should do. As the system gets flooded with sugar, insulin, whose job it is to regulate sugar and fat in the body, goes into overdrive.

The best way to get your body chemistry under control is by getting a grip on blood sugar, and the best way to do that, believe it or not, is to follow Mom's cardinal rule: Eat a healthy breakfast. If you initiate the glucose roller coaster first thing in the morning by going for a bagel with jam or, worse, a Danish and coffee, you will have set the stage for imbalance throughout the rest of the day.

Whether you skip breakfast, starting the day low on glucose, or you eat a highly refined, sugary breakfast that leads to a drop in blood sugar, your brain will be dogmatic about getting what it needs. It will crave sugar, and if you deny those cravings, the brain will go after your lean muscle for food. Talk about an energy drain on your body!

Studies show that people who eat breakfast are healthier. A balanced breakfast supports your blood sugar from the get-go, giving your brain a strong and steady supply of glucose. Breakfast sets a foundation for the day, spiritually and physiologically.

A Whole-Foods Plan

We all want to be fit. A lean and strong body looks better, feels better, and functions better than its unfit counterpart. The wonderful news about the program in this book is that it could very well help you lose weight by allowing your body to work efficiently, as it was meant to.

What I'm presenting is not a diet, however. My program relies on sound eating principles that will help you manage your weight, cardiovascular health, mood, and day-to-day performance. This solution is centered on a whole-foods approach to eating for wellness. A whole-foods plan emphasizes eating fresh, organic, local, and seasonal products. It emphasizes looking at food as both a pleasure and as something we should respect for giving the body what it really needs—in other words, it looks at food as fuel. It doesn't count calories, restrict fat intake, or present confusing food combinations and other limitations. It's simple.

With a whole-foods way of life, you steer clear of products laden with hormones, pesticides, and chemical preservatives, and you avoid refined sugar and bleached flour, as well as genetically modified foods (GMOs). Under a whole-foods plan, go for foods made of ingredients you can pronounce. Stick with foods whose ingredients come from the earth. Our bodies know what to do with real, natural, untreated foods because that's what we are designed to eat. The menu for a day of whole-foods could include two eggs with fresh spinach and tomato for breakfast; a midmorning snack of almonds; delicious poached salmon, brown rice, and kale for lunch; a piece of fresh fruit and some yogurt in the afternoon;

and roast turkey or even grilled chicken or fish with a fresh salad for dinner. (If organic foods aren't readily available in your area, you'll still benefit significantly from eating local, seasonal products, as those foods don't need to be treated with preservatives because they aren't being trucked across the country.)

Before you protest that organic foods cost more than nonorganic foods, keep this thought in mind: There is no greater expense in life than poor health. And if you buy and prepare organic foods, you'll enjoy eating this way so much that you won't spend as much money eating out. Plus, you won't be wasting money on items like soda and prepared desserts and snacks—all of which can add a lot to your grocery bill.

Eat with this in mind: These delicious foods will help stabilize body chemistry, manage blood sugar, calm inflammation, reduce cravings, feed the adrenal system, and help you reach and maintain a healthy weight. It's all about balance. By keeping blood sugar on an even keel, whole foods keep the body on an even keel. A whole-foods approach builds the body's stores of key nutrients, such as vitamin C, B vitamins, and minerals like magnesium, zinc, and potassium—all of which are building blocks for healthy adrenal and hormone function. If you can capture all this in a good diet and sustain it by making healthy choices every single day, you will have a handle on one of the greatest tools to mastering stress.

FEEDING YOUR SPIRIT

Food has always been ritualized. Historically, people worked hard for their food, and they had a religious appreciation for it. It's only recently that food has become big business, removed from nature and human effort. Food has become a product of convenience and entertainment more than nourishment, and it's something many of us take for granted. As a result, we don't have a conscious relationship with food. We don't think about what we put in our mouths, where it came from, and what it will do for us. A healthful way of life requires eating consciously, restoring significance and gratitude to our notions of food. After all, food does serve a purpose and is something we should still face with respect and be thankful for. A mindful approach to food is an essential and spiritual component of the whole-foods way.

The benefits of eating proactively include a psychological and spiritual boost that is as symbolic as it is chemical. Eating with intention alleviates stress because it makes you take the time to care for yourself. Each meal, each trip to the kitchen or the table, can be an opportunity for meditation in motion, a chance to bring you back to yourself. When you shop, shop with that in mind. Empower yourself through your dietary choices. Go through each day knowing that what you eat will keep you on top of your game. Face each meal consciously and spiritually. Develop a connection. Having a sense of control over what you're eating also helps you gain control over other areas of your life where you might feel like you're floundering.

The foods that are ideal for a healthy stress chemistry help support levels of serotonin, the body's natural antidepressant. They support the adrenal system so it can function optimally as daily stress occurs. When mind and body are fed well, you're going to live well. No matter what comes at you, you will have the wherewithal, physiologically and spiritually, to move through it and deal with it.

Food Combinations for Balance

The focus of my program is all about balance. To achieve balance, you need to enjoy foods rich in vitamins, nutrients, and amino acids that won't throw your cortisol and serotonin levels out of whack. This will help you stay calm and better manage stress. All meals should be macro-nutrient balanced, meaning that they should include a core protein, a low-glycemic (low sugar) complex carbohydrate, a healthy dose of beneficial fats, and vitamin- and mineral-rich fresh, green vegetables. At the same time, aim for a low-sodium, low-sugar diet. If your body feels funny after eating something (for example, you experience indigestion, a rash, lethargy, congestion, or difficulty breathing), don't eat it again.

This system is based on a triad. The core protein to aim for is a tryptophan-rich protein, such as in turkey or cottage cheese, for example, and some whole grains. Tryptophan, an amino acid, is one of the best ways to support serotonin in the body, but it isn't made available to the brain without the help of a complex carbohydrate such as brown rice or whole-grain toast.

By combining tryptophan-rich proteins with a complex carbohydrate, you will enjoy constant, soothing energy. The complex carbohydrate also provides the body with a sustained supply of glucose for the brain. Complex carbohydrates burn more slowly than simple carbs, and they keep blood glucose levels on an even keel. A tryptophan and complex carbohydrate combination, while helping you naturally build serotonin levels, will also help diminish your tendency to crave sugar, caffeine, and all the things that can create greater physiological stress.

This eating plan will be reinforced with glucose-friendly whole grains, fruits, and vegetables. Most high-glycemic foods tend to be refined, meaning that all key nutrients have been stripped away. For example, pasta, breads, and other foods made with white flour don't just spike blood sugar, they also fail to provide the body with essential vitamins and minerals. By the same token, foods with a low glycemic index tend to be nutrient dense, further supporting serotonin and dopamine, the neurotransmitters essential to stress management. (Dopamine is found in poultry and lean proteins rich in tyrosine. Like tryptophan, tyrosine is an amino acid. Unlike tryptophan, tyrosine-rich food can boost energy and metabolism most effectively if eaten alone or without carbohydrates.)

FOODS TO ENJOY

I chose the foods and meal plans here to help produce physical changes in the brain that can help prevent the exhaustion we often feel as a result of too much stress. The brain typically craves more sweets and carbohydrates during and after stressful times because it likes foods that can quickly raise serotonin levels. When serotonin levels are adequate, appetite usually decreases, which means you'll instinctively control the urge to eat everything in sight. The following lists of foods can guide you toward healthier, more balanced choices in eating. Aim to eat a variety of foods from each category. For example, just because you see your favorite fruit on the list, you still need to balance the intake of that fruit sugar with a lower glycemic protein or whole grain. Enjoy all the different foods listed and use the recipes that follow in Chapter 7 (see page 107) as creative ways to create dishes that utilize new foods and flavors.

Vegetables

* **Arame seaweed.** The kale of the ocean is a rich source of all kinds of minerals and B vitamins. It's also rich in lignates, which work to balance hormones. Since imbalanced hormones are behind insomnia and an inability to cope with stress, lignates are critical to a balanced diet.

* **Broccoli.** Part of the crucifer family, research has shown this supervegetable to be high in antioxidants and especially good for women with a high risk of breast cancer. Broccoli is also a great source of carotenoids, which are terrific for preventing macular degeneration. In addition, broccoli is high in folate, for heart health, and rich in indoles, to balance hormones. And broccoli's calcium content will help you sleep!

* **Cabbage.** Another member of the crucifer family, cabbage is strongly linked to cancer prevention. Cabbage is also a great source of vitamin C. Eat cabbage for its folate, which helps in heart disease prevention. It's also rich in the amino acid glutamine. This favorite food of the digestive tract helps produce healthy new cells and stave off ulcers.

* **Carrots.** This rich source of beta-carotene helps the body disarm destructive compounds that attack cells. These free-radical scavengers keep inflammation at bay.

* **Celery.** In Chinese medicine, celery has been used for centuries to treat high blood pressure. It's a very water-dense vegetable that's low in sugar, and it makes a very satisfying snack.

* **Greens (spinach, bib lettuce, butterleaf lettuce, dandelion greens).** Green leafies contain many beneficial elements, including phytochemicals—super plant-based compounds that protect against a variety of diseases, including cancer.

* **Kale.** Also a member of the crucifer family, kale has many of the benefits associated with broccoli. It's also particularly good for hormone support and is high in both vitamin C and calcium.

* **Shiitake mushrooms.** These delicate, aromatic mushrooms often found in Asian food are great for immune system support. In Chinese medicine, shiitake mushrooms are used as life or "chi" energy tonics. Studies show they are also good for cancer prevention.

* **Spinach (fresh or frozen).** Popeye's favorite food is rich in calcium, iron, and vitamin C.

* **Swiss chard.** Another terrific supervegetable, Swiss chard is calcium-rich and is an excellent source of tryptophan, as well as glutathion—an antioxidant that helps detoxify the liver.

Fruit

* **Apples.** Apples are a good source of flavonoids, which are key to breast health. They are also high in fiber; one apple has as much fiber as approximately 10 small salads. The apple peel is rich in quercitin, an anti-inflammatory nutrient good for respiratory stress.

* **Bananas.** A double-fisted defense against stress chemistry, bananas are rich in tryptophan and potassium. Sliced banana on toast with peanut butter offers great support for the neurotransmitters that encourage sleep and tranquility.

* **Blueberries.** These lovely berries are powerful antioxidants. They are also key to providing brain and memory support.

* **Dates.** These oft-overlooked fruits are high in fiber. Eat them fresh for the low-sugar version, and discover their subtle refreshment.

* **Grapefruit.** A great source of vitamin C and pectin, grapefruit is healthy for the digestive tract.

* **Lemons.** Rich in vitamin C, lemons are also great immunity boosters. Half a lemon squeezed into a glass of water first thing in the morning works as an effective internal cleanser.

* **Oranges.** The mother of all fruits high in vitamin C also has high levels of hesperidin, a flavonoid that fights cancer and heart disease.

* **Strawberries.** The peach of all berries, so to speak, the strawberry is high in antioxidants, especially one called ellagic acid, believed to be a great inhibitor of cancer.

Grains, Legumes

* **Brown rice.** Brown rice is the staple of the Asian diet, which is recognized as the healthiest diet in the world. It's also a great source of insoluble fiber. Because your body can't absorb this fiber, brown rice picks up cholesterol and pulls it right out as it moves through the body. This whole grain is great for bowel regularity. It's also rich in manganese, an important mineral for bone health and blood sugar regulation.

* **Lentils.** Easy, delicious, and power-packed, lentils are high in folate, magnesium, and fiber.

* **Oats.** Oats have been proven to lower blood cholesterol and promote heart health. They're also a great source of soluble fiber for digestive health. In addition, eat them for their magnesium, B vitamins, and tryptophan. (Because oats are a complex carbohydrate, you get the benefits of tryptophan by eating them alone!)

* **Whole grains (amaranth, kamut, millet, quinoa, wheat).** Whole grains are a great source of fiber and contain lots of disease-fighting compounds, including vitamin E, zinc, and folate, which lowers homocysteine, improving circulatory health. You'll find whole grains in breads, cereals, muffins, wheat bran, and wheat germ.

SUPPORT FROM DIETARY SUPPLEMENTS

I strongly believe that everyone can benefit from a good multivitamin. However, in addition to taking a multivitamin, there are instances when your body can use extra support. If you're under chronic stress or your diet is less than ideal, you could probably use additional amounts of key nutrients to nourish your body and mind. That's why I put together the following list of dietary supplements that I think are worthwhile.

Antioxidants. Antioxidants are thought to slow down the aging process, in addition to protecting the body against free-radical damage. Vitamin C (see the opposite page), vitamin E, the carotenoids (including beta carotene), vitamin A, selenium, zinc, flavonoids from purple grapes (found in juice and red wine), polyphenols from green tea, and ellagic acid are all part of the antioxidant family. Studies suggest that supplementing with a combination antioxidant product may be the best way to go.

Recommended daily amounts: vitamin E, 400 to 800 milligrams; beta carotene, 60 milligrams; selenium, 100 to 200 micrograms; zinc, 20 milligrams; and vitamin A, 5,000 IU (pregnant women should not take vitamin A beyond what is in their prenatal vitamin)

Calcium. Calcium is critical for maintaining optimal blood pressure and heart function, as well as for keeping our bones strong. When taken at bedtime, calcium may also be useful for treating insomnia.

Recommended daily amount: 1,000 milligrams

Essential fatty acids. Omega-3 fish oils, along with unrefined and organic flaxseed oil, provide essential fats that are lacking in many of our diets. Our bodies need these essential oils for storing energy and decreasing inflammation.

Recommended daily amount: 1 to 2 grams

Magnesium. Magnesium is another nutrient that is critical to energy production

Dairy, Soy

* **Milk.** Milk is high in tryptophan and calcium, two important nutrients for serotonin and melatonin support.

* **Soy milk.** Soy milk is high in calcium and provides anti-inflammatory beneficial fats.

* **Tofu.** This vegetarian food is high in calcium.

* **Yogurt, mozzarella cheese, and cottage cheese.** All of these are high in tryptophan and calcium.

in the body and is often overlooked in terms of its benefits to human health. Magnesium deficiency is actually fairly common today. This may predispose many people to the signs and symptoms of stress, as well as premenstrual syndrome and insomnia.

Recommended daily amount: 500 milligrams

Plant sterols. You can find plant sterols and sterolins in Moducare, an over-the-counter food supplement that is a safe and effective way to naturally support healthy cortisol levels.

Recommended daily amount: 60 milligrams

Vitamin B family. The family of B vitamins has historically been viewed as the solution to stress, and for good reason—these vitamins are involved in energy metabolism in the body and provide vital nutrition for the brain and endocrine system. Pyridoxine (vitamin B_6) is especially important for maintaining hormonal balance, as it's essential for the production of

neurotransmitters in the brain. Pantothenic acid (vitamin B_5) plays a major role in the manufacture of adrenal hormones.

Recommended daily amounts: 50 to 100 milligrams each of B_5 and B_6

Vitamin C. Vitamin C is a powerful antioxidant that's another vital contributor to the manufacture of key hormones and neurotransmitters. Because our bodies don't produce vitamin C on their own, we need to get this nutrient from our diet. The recommended dietary allowance of vitamin C was established merely to prevent scurvy, but most of us could benefit from an additional dose of this vitamin.

Recommended daily amount: 1 to 2 grams (in divided doses).

Zinc. Zinc stores may become depleted during long-term stress, which wears down a person's immune system. For best absorption in the body, don't take zinc with high fiber foods.

Recommended daily amount: 20 milligrams

Fish

❊ **Halibut, salmon, and mackerel.** Fish in general are great sources of omega-3 fatty acids, which are beneficial to the heart and immune system as well as to memory, brain function, and emotional well-being. The tryptophan in fish helps support key neurotransmitters. Because of a reported connection between fish consumption and mercury poisoning, though, it's best to alternate fish with other proteins. Pacific halibut, salmon, and mackerel tend to have the lowest mercury content and highest omega-3 concentrations, so I've chosen to list only those types here.

HERBAL STRESS RELIEF

You can also turn to herbs, particularly adaptogenic herbs, for help with stress relief. As the name suggests, an adaptogenic herb adapts to work where it's most needed. For example, when you're stressed, it helps to calm you down, and when you're dragging, it can give you an energy boost. Your best bet it to take these herbs in the morning or during the day when you need extra support.

Ashwagandha. This is an ayurvedic herb that's been used for centuries to help prevent stress and exhaustion.

Recommended daily amount:
500 to 1,000 milligrams

Cordyceps. This herb has been called an aphrodisiac, but that's not why I'm recommending it. It helps the body develop strength, increases longevity, and provides support for the immune system.

Recommended daily amount:
2 to 4 grams

Holy basil. This is can be beneficial for mental fatigue. Preliminary research also suggests that it may help lower elevated cortisol levels.

Recommended daily amount:
800 milligrams

Panax ginseng. Panax ginseng has typically been used for mental and physical fatigue and may be useful when you're trying to get rid of nervous energy.

Recommended daily amount:
100 milligrams standardized extract

Rhodiola. Rhodiola is perhaps best known for exciting the nervous system, improving work performance, easing depression, and providing a bit of an energy boost. It's just starting to gain popularity in the United States but has been used for some time with considerable success in Europe and Asia.

Recommended daily amount:
200 milligrams

Meat, Poultry

* **Chicken and turkey.** Both of these fowl are great sources of tryptophan (turkey has three to four times the tryptophan that chicken does), which is a building block for both serotonin and melatonin, a supporter of proper brain function.

* **Eggs.** Eggs are rich in omega-3 fatty acids and are good sources of tryptophan. The protein in eggs helps keep blood sugar stable.

* **Lean beef.** Lean beef provides vitamin B_5.

Nuts, Seeds, and Oils

✳ **Almonds and almond butter.** Almond butter improves cholesterol by bringing down bad cholesterol (LDL) and raising good cholesterol (HDL).

✳ **Flaxseed.** Flaxseed is rich in omega-3 fatty acids, which protect the heart and can prevent cancer. Flaxseed is also a beneficial anti-inflammatory. Sprinkle flaxseed on oatmeal, rice, or salads.

✳ **Hazelnuts.** These nuts are an especially good source of omega-3 fatty acids, which help lower cholesterol.

✳ **Olive oil.** Olive oil is rich in monounsaturated fats.

✳ **Peanuts and cashews.** Peanuts are high in tryptophan, while cashews are rich in monounsaturated (beneficial) fats.

✳ **Pumpkin seeds.** Pumpkin seeds are mineral dense, rich in zinc and magnesium, and particularly good for stress management and boosting immune function. They are also great for heart health.

BODY-PLEASING MEAL PLANS

The meal plans that I've put together contain recipes that are designed to be fun as well as supportive of your body chemistry. Breakfast sets the tone for blood sugar balance, while lunch is a time to focus and recharge your physical, mental, and emotional batteries. Dinner is a time of recovery and balance, restoration and relaxation.

I've also broken the plans down into meals that are simple and quick to make, for those days when time is short, and meals that are a bit more elaborate, for when you can take your time in the kitchen.

Breakfast

Cold, simple, and quick

* "Be Alive" Peach Smoothie (page 108)

* Banana Bran Almond Butter Square (page 110)

* Morning Granola Parfait (page 112)

Warm and more elaborate

* Nutty French Toast (page 111)

* Vegetable Frittata (page 114)

Lunch

Cold, simple, and quick

* Mixed field greens with salmon

* Open-Face Turkey Veggie Sandwich (page 120)

Warm and more elaborate

* Seared Tofu (page 117) with steamed broccoli

* Salmon Burger (page 118) on a whole-grain bun with steamed spinach

Dinner

Cold, simple, and quick

* Pasta Chicken Salad (page 122)

* Greens with crumbled turkey bacon, avocado, sliced chicken, hard-boiled egg, and honey-mustard dressing

Warm and more elaborate

* Easy Veggie Chili (page 124) with whole-grain roll or Cornbread Muffin (page 131)

* Rosemary Trout (page 129) with brown basmati rice and steamed kale

Snacks

Cold, simple, and quick

* 1 Boundless Energy Bar (page 130)

* ½ cup Sweet and Spicy Nuts (page 135)

* Raw nuts or seeds (¼ cup)

* 1 piece fresh fruit, such as an apple or pear

* String cheese, ½ cup cottage cheese, or 1 cup yogurt

Warm and more elaborate

* 1 Gingerbread Muffin (page 132)

* 1 cup warm oatmeal with cinnamon and ¼ cup milk or soy milk

* 1 baked apple with ½ teaspoon cinnamon and 1 teaspoon honey

7

Stress-Reducing Recipes

Are you eating for your health?

The following recipes were designed and selected specifically to support energy and equilibrium in the body. These recipes are rich in key nutrients such as vitamin B$_6$ and fiber and low in simple sugars—a combination that can help cause a decline in stress hormones in your body. I also tried to choose recipes that are fun and not too time-consuming to prepare.

"BE ALIVE" PEACH SMOOTHIE

Peaches are one of the few low-fat foods that naturally supply healthy amounts of vitamin E. This smoothie also packs potassium, fiber, and pectin to support a healthy heart—and a more energized you.

> 2 cups soy milk
> 2 tablespoons low-fat vanilla yogurt
> 1 cup peeled and sliced peaches
> ¼ cup sliced strawberries
> 1 banana, sliced

Put all the ingredients in a blender and blend until smooth. For a thicker smoothie, use frozen fruit instead of fresh.

Optional: Add 2 tablespoons of your favorite protein powder for a 12- to 14-gram protein boost per serving.

Serves 2.

Per serving: 189 calories; 5 g fat (23% calories from fat); 9 g protein; 31 g carbohydrates; 7 g fiber; 1 mg cholesterol; 40 mg sodium

"BE ALIVE" PEACH SMOOTHIE

BANANA BRAN ALMOND BUTTER SQUARES

These delicious breakfast squares are high in B vitamins, protein, and fiber, to help jump-start your day in a balanced way. The vitamin B_6 content may also help nourish brain hormones, promoting a sense of calm and well-being.

1 cup whole-wheat flour
½ cup oat flour
¼ cup wheat germ
¼ cup ground flaxseed
¼ cup brown sugar, packed
½ teaspoon baking soda
1 teaspoon baking powder
¼ teaspoon salt
1½ teaspoons cinnamon
1 cup soy milk
2 eggs
1 ripe banana, mashed
½ cup almond butter

Preheat the oven to 375°F. Lightly grease an 8½ × 8½-inch baking pan. In a medium bowl, combine the whole-wheat flour, oat flour, wheat germ, flaxseed, sugar, baking soda, baking powder, salt, and cinnamon. Mix well.

In another bowl, combine the soy milk, eggs, banana, and almond butter.

Fold the wet ingredients into the dry ingredients just until the dry ingredients are moistened. Pour into the prepared pan. Bake for 25 to 35 minutes or until brown on top. Cool in the pan on a wire rack. When cool, cut into bars.

Makes 12 bars.

Per serving: 206 calories; 10 g fat (39% calories from fat); 8 g protein; 27 g carbohydrates; 6 g fiber; 31 mg cholesterol; 194 mg sodium

NUTTY FRENCH TOAST

A healthy twist on an old classic, Nutty French Toast cooks up fast and provides a good dose of fiber and essential fats, plus the complex carbohydrates you need to get you moving in the morning.

2 large eggs
½ teaspoon vanilla extract
½ cup soy or low-fat milk
¼ teaspoon cinnamon
¼ teaspoon nutmeg
⅓ cup ground almonds
⅓ cup rolled oats
4 slices French bread
Butter

Preheat a nonstick griddle over medium heat. Crack the eggs into a pie pan, add the vanilla, and whisk until smooth. Whisk in the milk, cinnamon, and nutmeg until well blended.

Spread the almonds and oats in another pie plate and mix well.

Coat both sides of each piece of bread with the egg mixture. Then coat both sides of each piece of bread with the almond and oat mixture.

Melt some butter on the hot griddle and place the coated bread on the griddle. Fry over medium heat for about 4 minutes on each side. Serve the French toast hot with real maple syrup.

Serves 2.

Per serving: 408 calories; 19 g fat (41% calories from fat); 20 g protein; 42 g carbohydrates; 6 g fiber; 187 mg cholesterol; 370 mg sodium

MORNING GRANOLA PARFAIT

This homemade granola plus yogurt parfait is such a treat that you'll forget how healthy it is for you. (It contains essential fats, calcium, fiber, and protein.)

⅓ cup chopped strawberries
⅓ cup chopped kiwi
2 tablespoons granola (see recipe below)
1 cup low-fat yogurt
2 tablespoons sliced almonds, toasted

Beginning with the strawberries and kiwis, alternate layers of fruit, granola, and ¼ cup yogurt in 2 goblets or parfait glasses. End with fruit. Top with almonds.

Serves 2.

Per serving: 234 calories; 7 g fat (27% calories from fat); 9 g protein; 36 g carbohydrates; 3 g fiber; 2 mg cholesterol; 82 mg sodium (Note: Analysis does not include dried fruit)

GRANOLA

3 cups rolled oats
½ cup wheat germ
½ cup chopped almonds
¼ cup sunflower seeds
¼ cup shredded dried coconut
¼ cup canola oil
¼ cup maple syrup
1 teaspoon almond extract
Dried fruits (currants, blueberries, raisins)

Preheat the oven to 350°F. In a large bowl, mix together the oats, wheat germ, almonds, sunflower seeds, and coconut. Add the oil, syrup, and almond extract, and stir until well mixed. Divide the mixture in half and spread evenly across 2 ungreased cookie sheets. Bake for about 20 minutes or until slightly browned. Allow to cool, add the dried fruit, and mix again. Store granola in an airtight container.

MORNING GRANOLA PARFAIT

VEGETABLE FRITTATA

Get in a few servings of greens before you head out the door with this balanced protein- and fiber-rich breakfast. This veggie frittata will leave you satisfied and energized, ready to begin the day with a positive outlook.

1 cup sliced shiitake mushrooms
1 large onion, thinly sliced
1 clove garlic, minced
1 tablespoon olive oil
½ cup broccoli florets
1 cup spinach leaves
½ cup chopped zucchini
2 tomatoes, cut in half and sliced
12 large eggs
Salt and pepper, to taste
1 tablespoon fresh rosemary, to taste

Preheat the oven to 450°F. Heat a cast-iron skillet over medium heat. Sauté the mushrooms, onion, and garlic in olive oil in the skillet until the onions are translucent. Add the broccoli, spinach, zucchini, and tomatoes to the skillet, and stir-fry for an additional 5 minutes.

In a separate bowl, beat the eggs and season to taste with the salt, pepper, and rosemary. Pour the eggs over the vegetables. Bake for about 20 minutes, until the eggs are firm and puffed through the center of the frittata. (Depending on your oven, you may need to adjust the cooking temperature.)

Serves 6.

Per serving: 343 calories; 29 g fat (78% calories from fat); 12 g protein; 6 g carbohydrates; 1 g fiber; 374 mg cholesterol; 120 mg sodium

FISH FAJITAS

Fish is food for the brain. This recipe is a rich source of essential fats, protein, and phytonutrients that support optimum nutrition.

> 1 ½ tablespoons olive oil
> 1 ½ cups green bell pepper strips
> ¾ cup thinly sliced onion
> 1 ½ pounds cod fillets (roughy or grouper would work, too),
>   cut into ½-inch strips
> ⅓ cup beer
> ¼ teaspoon salt
> ⅛ teaspoon black pepper
> 4 flour tortillas

Heat the oil in a large nonstick skillet over medium-high heat. Add the bell pepper, onion, and fish; sauté for 3 minutes. Add the beer. Cook for 5 minutes or until almost all the liquid has evaporated and the fish flakes easily with a fork. Remove from the heat and sprinkle with salt and pepper. Divide the fish mixture evenly among the tortillas, and roll up. Serve with ½ cup of Mango-Avocado Salsa (see page 116) or the topping of your choice.

Serves 4.

Per serving: 447 calories; 11 g fat (24% calories from fat); 37 g protein; 46 g carbohydrates; 3 g fiber; 73 mg cholesterol; 695 mg sodium

MANGO-AVOCADO SALSA

Mangos contain large amounts of vitamin C and beta-carotene, both powerful anti-oxidants. Both mango and avocado are loaded with fiber. In fact, one mango supplies nearly 6 grams of fiber—more than you'd get in one cup of cooked oat bran. If you are concerned about the fat content of avocado, you may want to rethink your fat fears. Avocados are rich in oleic acid, which can actually help *lower* cholesterol! And did I mention potassium and folate? Two more reasons to love avocado and ways to decrease your risk of heart disease.

    1 cup peeled and cubed mango
    1 cup cubed avocado
    2 tablespoons lemon or lime juice
    2 tablespoons chopped fresh cilantro
    1 cup cherry tomatoes, halved

Mix all the ingredients together. Chill before serving.

Serves 4.

Per serving: 125 calories; 8 g fat (52% calories from fat); 2 g protein; 15 g carbohydrates; 3 g fiber; 0 mg cholesterol; 10 mg sodium

SEARED TOFU

Tofu isn't just for vegetarians. It's an excellent source of phytonutrients and protein that can be enjoyed by omnivores anytime.

    1 tablespoon sesame oil
    ½ teaspoon dried red pepper flakes
    1 teaspoon minced fresh ginger
    1 clove garlic, minced
    1 tablespoon tamari soy sauce
    16 ounces tofu, cut into triangles*

Heat the sesame oil in a frying pan and add the pepper flakes, ginger, and garlic. Stir over medium heat for 2 to 3 minutes. Sprinkle the tofu with half of the soy sauce on each side. Pan sear the tofu in the herbs for about 3 minutes on each side, or until lightly browned.

*To cut into triangles, first cut into ½-inch rectangles, then slice diagonally into triangles.

Serves 4.

Per serving: 121 calories; 9 g fat (61% calories from fat); 10 g protein; 3 g carbohydrates; 1 g fiber; 0 mg cholesterol; 260 mg sodium

SALMON BURGERS

Rich in omega-3 fatty acids and vitamins B_6, B_{12}, and niacin, these salmon burgers are a treat that can be enjoyed on their own or paired with a whole-grain bun, brown rice, or a salad of field greens. Salmon tends to be very balancing for the mind and body and is a good choice for lunch when your afternoon will present a mental challenge.

> 1 pound Alaskan salmon
> 2 tablespoons lemon juice
> 1½ teaspoons Dijon mustard
> ¾ cup cooked brown rice
> ½ cup sliced green onions
> 2 eggs

Place all the ingredients in a food processor and pulse until well blended but not liquefied. Form the mixture into 4 patties and grill or broil them until golden brown on each side and heated through. Serve each burger on a bun with lettuce, tomato slices, and condiments as desired.

Serves 4.

Per serving: 214 calories; 7 g fat (31% calories from fat); 25 g protein; 10 g carbohydrates; 1 g fiber; 62 mg cholesterol; 682 mg sodium

SALMON BURGERS

OPEN-FACE TURKEY VEGGIE SANDWICH

This tasty sandwich contains healthy amounts of tryptophan, found in the turkey. The bell peppers are an excellent source of vitamin C. The pumpernickel bread is naturally high in fiber and rates low on the glycemic index, which is a plus for managing healthy blood sugar levels.

1 cup bell peppers, sliced (use a mix of red, green, and yellow)
½ cup thinly sliced onions
4 slices pumpernickel bread, toasted
2 teaspoons mayonnaise
2 teaspoons stone-ground mustard
1 pound cooked turkey breast, sliced
2 ounces Monterey Jack cheese

Preheat the oven to 350°F. (You could also prepare this recipe in a toaster oven, if you prefer.) Spray a 12-inch skillet with nonstick cooking spray; heat over medium-high heat. Stir-fry the peppers and onions until they're tender—about 5 to 8 minutes. Remove the vegetables from the skillet.

Top each slice of bread with about ½ teaspoon each of mayonnaise and mustard. Divide the turkey into four servings. Top the mayonnaise and mustard with turkey, followed by the bell peppers and onions and a thin slice of cheese. Heat for 5 minutes.

Serves 4.

Per serving: 297 calories; 10 g fat (31% calories from fat); 31 g protein; 19 g carbohydrates; 3 g fiber; 76 mg cholesterol; 558 mg sodium

OPEN-FACE TURKEY VEGGIE SANDWICH

PASTA CHICKEN SALAD

This dish has it all—tryptophan, vitamin B_6, magnesium, fiber, iron. It's a great combination of ingredients for a meal that satisfies on many levels.

2 cups pasta shells
1½ cups cooked and cubed chicken
⅓ cup chicken broth
2 tablespoons olive oil
2 tablespoons lemon juice
1 tablespoon chopped fresh tarragon or basil
1 teaspoon sugar
½ teaspoon salt
¼ teaspoon pepper
3 cups bite-size pieces of baby spinach greens
1 small red or green bell pepper, cut into ½-inch pieces
¼ cup green onions, chopped
Small amount of feta or shaved Parmesan cheese (optional)

Cook the pasta as directed on the package. Drain, rinse with cold water, and drain again. Combine the pasta and chicken in large bowl.

In a container with a lid, combine the broth, olive oil, lemon juice, tarragon or basil, sugar, salt, and pepper. Shake well. Stir the dressing into the pasta-chicken mixture. Cover and refrigerate for at least 2 hours. Toss the pasta-chicken mixture with the spinach, bell pepper, and green onions just before serving, and garnish with the cheese, if using.

Serves 4.

Per serving: 385 calories; 18 g fat (41% calories from fat); 27 g protein; 29 g carbohydrates; 3 g fiber; 162 mg cholesterol; 1,017 mg sodium

CHICKEN, SPINACH, AND MACADAMIA NUT ENCHILADAS

Such diverse ingredients turn this basic Mexican fare into a gourmet wellness meal. Feel free to omit the cheese if you're looking to reduce fat or calories.

    1 pound fresh tomatillos
    2 cloves garlic, peeled
    1 jalapeño pepper, seeded and diced
    ⅓ cup diced green chilies
    2 tablespoons cilantro leaves
    2 tablespoons onion, chopped
    1⅓ cup sour cream
    ⅓ cup plain yogurt
    1 tablespoon honey
    ¼ teaspoon salt
    6 corn tortillas
    2 cups cooked shredded chicken
    1 cup cooked spinach
    1 cup shredded Monterey Jack cheese
    1 cup macadamia nuts
    ½ cup green onion, diced

Preheat the oven to 350°F. Remove the husks from the tomatillos, rinse the fruit, and chop them into pieces. Place in a saucepan, cover with water, and simmer until they're tender, about 5 to 7 minutes. Drain and discard the liquid.

Place the tomatillos, garlic, jalapeño, chilies, cilantro, onion, sour cream, yogurt, honey, and salt in a food processor and purée. Soften the tortillas either by frying them on both sides in a small amount of vegetable oil or by heating them according to the package directions. Then place about 2 tablespoons each of chicken, spinach, and tomatilla sauce, plus 1 tablespoon of cheese, in the center of each tortilla. Add about 2 teaspoons of chopped macadamia nuts to each tortilla. Place the filled enchiladas in a greased 9 × 12-inch baking dish, and pour the remaining sauce over the top. Sprinkle with the remaining cheese and green onions. Bake until heated through, about 20 minutes.

Serves 6.

Per serving: 441 calories; 27 g fat (53% calories from fat); 26 g protein; 27 g carbohydrates; 5 g fiber; 64 mg cholesterol; 318 mg sodium

EASY VEGGIE CHILI

Unlike many chili recipes, this one is quick and easy. It's also a wonderful source of phytonutrients, fiber, folate, magnesium, and potassium. Serve it over brown rice or with a cornbread muffin.

2 teaspoons olive oil
1 cup chopped onion
½ cup chopped green bell pepper
½ cup chopped red bell pepper
1 medium zucchini, chopped into quarters
2 cloves garlic, chopped
2 cans (15 ounces each) pinto beans, rinsed and drained
2 cans (14½ ounces each) salsa tomatoes with diced green chiles, undrained
3 teaspoons chili powder

Heat the oil in a Dutch oven over medium-high heat. Cook the onion, green and red peppers, zucchini, and garlic in the oil, stirring frequently, until the onion is tender. Stir in the beans, tomatoes, and chili powder; reduce heat. Cover and simmer for 20 minutes.

Serving suggestion: Serve with shredded cheese, minced onions, and low-fat sour cream.

Serves 4.

Per serving: 300 calories; 7 g fat (19% calories from fat); 14 g protein; 50 g carbohydrates; 13 g fiber; 6 mg cholesterol; 1,200 mg sodium*

* You can reduce the sodium content by using unsalted beans and tomatoes.

EASY VEGGIE CHILI

PORTOBELLO MUSHROOMS WITH ROASTED ASPARAGUS

This vegetarian entrée is a nutrient powerhouse, packed with selenium, riboflavin, niacin, iron, potassium, folate, and fiber.

> 1 bunch green onions
> 2 large portobello mushroom caps, sliced
> ¼ cup walnut oil
> 1½ pounds asparagus spears
> 3 teaspoons balsamic vinegar
> 1 teaspoon sea salt
> 1 teaspoon black pepper
> ½ teaspoon basil

Preheat the oven to 450°F. Toss the green onions and mushroom slices with half of the walnut oil. Spread the onions and mushrooms on the bottom of a baking dish and roast for about 10 minutes. Toss the asparagus with the remaining oil and add to the roasting pan. Sprinkle the balsamic vinegar, salt, pepper, and basil over the top. Roast for another 10 minutes, or until the veggies are crisp and delicious.

Serves 8.

Per serving: 80 calories; 7 g fat (74% calories from fat); 2 g protein; 4 g carbohydrates; 1 g fiber; 0 mg cholesterol; 238 mg sodium

PORTOBELLO MUSHROOMS WITH ROASTED ASPARAGUS

PINON-AND-CORN ENCRUSTED HALIBUT WITH MANGO-AVOCADO SALSA

This is one of the Rouse family favorites. The Mango-Avocado Salsa (see page 116) really makes this a wonderful dish and it adds a ton of vitamin C and fiber to the already nutrient-dense meal.

    4 halibut fillets, 4 to 6 ounces each
    1 cup rice flour
    2 eggs
    4 corn tortillas, torn into small pieces
    1 cup pine nuts
    1 tablespoon dried thyme
    1 teaspoon sea salt
    1 teaspoon black pepper
    1 tablespoon olive oil

Preheat the oven to 350°F. Skin and rinse the halibut fillets, and set them aside. Place the rice flour on a plate (this is for dipping fillets in). In a small, shallow dish or bowl, whisk the eggs together.

In a food processor, place the tortilla pieces, pine nuts, thyme, salt, and pepper. Process until the mixture is finely crumbled. Place the mixture on a plate (this is also for dipping fillets in).

Create a sort of assembly line: Dip the fillet in the flour, then in the egg, and finally in the pine nut mixture.

Heat the olive oil in a large skillet over medium-high heat. Add the fillets so that each one completely comes in contact with the bottom of the skillet. (You want to toast or brown the crust.) Sear each side for about 5 minutes. Remove the fillets to an oven-proof baking dish and bake an additional 15 to 20 minutes. Serve ½ cup of Mango-Avocado Salsa over the fish.

Serves 4.

Per serving: 693 calories; 34 g fat (43% calories from fat); 37 g protein; 64 g carbohydrates; 7 g fiber; 126 mg cholesterol; 602 mg sodium

ROSEMARY TROUT

Rosemary is a powerful antioxidant and when steamed, as in this recipe, it produces a magnificent and soothing aroma. Enjoy the unique flavor of this dish while also benefiting from the trout's healthy fats.

    4 trout fillets, ½ pound each
    ½ teaspoon salt
    ¼ teaspoon pepper
    4 sprigs rosemary (each about 3 inches long)
    4 thin slices lemon
    4 tablespoons olive oil
    Lemon wedges

Heat coals or a gas grill for direct heat, or preheat the oven to 350°F. Place each fillet on a piece of aluminum foil large enough to cover the fillet entirely, or place all fillets in an oven-safe glass pan coated lightly with nonstick cooking spray. Sprinkle the fillets with the salt and pepper. Place 1 sprig of rosemary and 1 slice of lemon on each fillet. Drizzle 1 tablespoon of olive oil over each fillet. Wrap the fish up, if using aluminum foil.

Grill the fish about 4 inches from medium heat for 20 to 25 minutes, turning once, until the fish flakes easily with a fork. Alternately, bake for 15 to 20 minutes and brush with additional oil every 7 to 10 minutes.

Serve the fish with the lemon wedges.

Serves 4.

Per serving: 353 calories; 15 g fat (38% calories from fat); 47 g protein; 8 g carbohydrates; 2 g fiber; 134 mg cholesterol; 340 mg sodium

BOUNDLESS ENERGY BARS

When you need a pick-me-up, these bars are the way to go. They travel well in wax paper or plastic wrap, so you can take them with you to enjoy anytime.

1 cup rolled oats
1 cup of your favorite crunchy cereal
¼ cup sesame seeds
1½ cups chopped dried apricots
1 cup raisins
¼ cup chopped almonds
¼ cup wheat germ
½ cup protein powder
1 tablespoon butter or canola oil
¾ cup brown rice syrup
½ cup peanut butter
1 teaspoon cinnamon

Preheat the oven to 350°F. Lightly spray a 9 × 13-inch pan with nonstick cooking spray.

Spread the oats, cereal, and sesame seeds out on an ungreased cookie sheet and toast for about 10 minutes. Cool slightly, then transfer from the cookie sheet to a large mixing bowl. Add the apricots, raisins, almonds, wheat germ, and protein powder. (Separate the apricots and raisins so they're not stuck in clumps.) Mix well.

In a saucepan over medium heat, melt the butter or heat the oil. Add the brown rice syrup, stirring until bubbly. Mix in the peanut butter and cinnamon. Pour into the dry ingredients, and quickly mix together and transfer into the prepared pan. Press the mixture into the pan and refrigerate for at least 4 hours. Cut into 12 bars and wrap each one separately in wax paper; store in the refrigerator.

Makes 12 bars.

Per serving: 283 calories; 10 g fat (31% calories from fat); 7 g protein; 46 g carbohydrates; 4 g fiber; 3 mg cholesterol; 56 mg sodium

CORNBREAD MUFFINS

These muffins are simple, yet high in fiber and vitamin C. They pair well with many of the entrées listed here.

1 cup cornmeal
1 cup whole-wheat flour
½ teaspoon sea salt
1 teaspoon baking powder
⅓ teaspoon baking soda
¼ cup canola oil or butter, melted
¼ cup honey
1 cup buttermilk or soy milk
1 egg

Preheat the oven to 325°F. Grease or line 10 muffin tins. Combine the cornmeal, flour, salt, baking powder, and baking soda in a bowl. Combine the butter or oil, honey, milk, and egg in a separate bowl. Mix the wet ingredients into the dry ones until they're moistened. Fill the muffin tins evenly and bake for 20 to 25 minutes, or until lightly browned.

Makes 10 muffins.

Per serving: 182 calories; 7 g fat (32% calories from fat); 4 g protein; 28 g carbohydrates; 3 g fiber; 20 mg cholesterol; 217 mg sodium

GINGERBREAD MUFFINS

I love ginger because of its wonderful anti-inflammatory qualities. These muffins are what
I consider "low drama" because they aren't too harsh in terms of sugar content—
meaning they won't give you that sugar high that leaves you destined to crash later—and
the whole-grain flour makes them high in fiber.

¼ cup packed brown sugar
½ cup molasses
⅓ cup soy milk
⅓ cup applesauce, unsweetened
1 egg
2 cups whole-wheat flour
1 teaspoon baking powder
1 teaspoon ground ginger
½ teaspoon salt
½ teaspoon baking soda
½ teaspoon ground cinnamon
¼ teaspoon ground cloves

Preheat the oven to 400°F. Grease the bottoms only of 12 medium muffin cups, each
2½ × 1¼ inches, or line each cup with a paper baking cup. Use a spoon to beat
the brown sugar, molasses, soy milk, applesauce, and egg together in a large bowl.
Stir in the flour, baking powder, ginger, salt, baking soda, cinnamon, and cloves just
until moistened.

Divide the batter evenly among the muffin cups. Bake for 18 to 20 minutes or until a
toothpick inserted in the center of a muffin comes out clean. Immediately remove
from pan to wire rack. Serve warm if desired.

Makes 12 muffins.

Per serving: 133 calories; 1 g fat (6% calories from fat); 3 g protein; 30 g carbohydrates; 3 g fiber; 16 mg
cholesterol; 195 mg sodium

GINGERBREAD MUFFINS

NUTTY OATMEAL COOKIES

The soluble fiber in oats makes these cookies wonderfully satisfying and filling. Oats can also help lower blood sugar—meaning these cookies are great for a healthy afternoon treat. Sucanat, the first ingredient listed below, is evaporated sugar cane juice that contains naturally occurring molasses. The benefit to using sucanat, as opposed to white or brown sugar, is that it still contains some of the actual nutrients from the sugar cane.

⅔ cup sucanat
⅓ cup maple sugar
¼ cup ghee, softened
½ cup applesauce (unsweetened or cinnamon)
2 eggs
1½ teaspoons vanilla
1½ teaspoons ground cinnamon
1 teaspoon baking soda
½ teaspoon baking powder
½ teaspoon salt
3 cups oats
1 cup whole-wheat flour
½ cup walnuts
½ cup raisins or chocolate chips (optional)

Preheat the oven to 375°F. Beat the sucanat, maple sugar, ghee, applesauce, eggs, and vanilla together in a large bowl. In a separate bowl, stir together the cinnamon, baking soda, baking powder, salt, oats, flour, and walnuts. Slowly add the dry ingredients to the wet and mix with a wooden spoon until just moistened. Stir in the raisins or chocolate chips, if using.

Line a cookie sheet with parchment paper or lightly coat it with nonstick spray. Drop rounded tablespoons of dough about 2 inches apart onto the sheet. Bake for 9 to 11 minutes or until light brown. Cool slightly on the cookie sheet, then remove to a wire rack.

Makes 30 cookies.

Per cookie: 82 calories; 2 g fat (22% calories from fat); 2 g protein; 15 g carbohydrates; 2 g fiber; 0 mg cholesterol; 104 mg sodium

SWEET AND SPICY NUTS

You'll find a little sugar, a little spice, and everything nice in this nutty combination. Snacking on these nuts can be addictive, so use good judgment and try not to eat the entire batch in one sitting. The essential fats are great for you, but nuts should, like all foods, be eaten in moderation.

1 cup almonds
1 cup walnuts
3 tablespoons sugar
1 teaspoon salt
½ teaspoon ground black pepper
1 teaspoon cinnamon
½ teaspoon curry powder or Cajun seasoning
1 pinch ground cloves
¼ teaspoon ground cumin

Preheat the oven to 350°F. Place the almonds and walnuts on a large baking tray. Bake for 5 to 10 minutes or until the nuts are golden and crisp. Remove from the oven and let cool.

Combine the sugar, salt, pepper, cinnamon, curry powder or Cajun seasoning, cloves, and cumin in a small bowl and mix well. Heat a large frying pan over medium heat and add the nuts. Sprinkle the spice mixture over the nuts. Cook the nuts, stirring frequently for 5 minutes or until they turn golden and are coated with the mixture. Remove from the heat. Spread on a lightly oiled baking sheet to cool.

Serves 6.

Per serving: 251 calories; 21 g fat (69% calories from fat); 8 g protein; 12 g carbohydrates; 3 g fiber; 0 mg cholesterol; 323 mg sodium

THUMBPRINT COOKIES

Eight simple ingredients make up these nutrient-dense cookies. Containing essential fats, fiber, protein, and phytonutrients, these cookies are as pleasing to the eye as they are to the tummy and brain.

1 cup whole-wheat flour
1 cup ground oats
1 cup ground almonds
¼ teaspoon salt
½ teaspoon cinnamon
½ cup canola oil
½ cup maple syrup
5 tablespoons strawberry jam

Preheat the oven to 350°F. Add the flour, oats, almonds, salt, and cinnamon to a blender or food processor. Blend or process until the ingredients are well mixed. Transfer to a large mixing bowl. In a separate bowl, mix together the oil and maple syrup. Add the liquids to the flour mixture, and mix well with a wooden spoon.

Shape the dough into walnut-size balls. Place the balls about 1 inch apart on an ungreased cookie sheet. Press your thumb into the center of each cookie to make an indentation. Add about ½ teaspoon of jam to the center of each cookie. Bake for about 10 minutes or until light brown.

Makes about 30 cookies.

Per cookie: 117 calories; 7 g fat (50% calories from fat); 2 g protein; 13 g carbohydrates; 2 g fiber; 0 mg cholesterol; 20 mg sodium

THUMBPRINT COOKIES

8

Short-Term Remedies

How will you handle acute stress?

Acute stress—stress that just springs up on you—is often caused by an unexpected scare or fright, such as an alarm going off, a loud noise, or accidentally dropping a glass. When faced with an acute stressor, the most important thing to remember is that you have it within you to respond in a calm and healthy way (assuming the stressor is not life-threatening). Remember that an unmanaged stress response will drive you out of balance. Be committed to handling stress proactively, one challenge at a time. Whether through breathing, meditation, or yoga, you have the tools to change any situation and its impact on your life. You can face life in peace, no matter what it throws at you.

The goal of this chapter is to provide you with short-term solutions for dealing with acute stress. What follows are some simple and very effective practices you can do that will change your state from one of frantic behavior and random aggression to a sense of empowerment and control. If you take the time for just one of these techniques the next time you face something stressful, you'll be on a course toward healing.

Use each stressor as an opportunity to return to mindfulness, a chance to remember who you are and get back in touch with your center. You can use stress to rediscover peace. Instead of living on the defensive, your life will assume a position of balance and harmony. Once you get to that place, you will be able to move through any previously perceived difficulties with a sense of well-being and centeredness. Everything around you will fall into alignment, and good things will start to come your way. Being open and receptive instead of closed and defensive is the best way to invite luck, abundance, and good fortune into your life.

YOUR FIRST RESPONSE

Taking slow, easy breaths should be your very first response to acute stress because slow breathing will keep your stress response from kicking into high gear. Breathing deeply is one of the best ways to change the atmosphere inside your body from one of calamity and chaos to one of harmony.

The first thing you can do in the face of acute or unexpected stress is to gasp or start breathing in short, frantic blasts, followed by shallow breathing. This is a natural reaction to stress; it's what we do. Accept it as an early sign that your stress response has been initiated, and check yourself. Ask if the response is necessary, and if not, bring your breath back to your belly.

This is the simplest, most effective way to disengage the stress response. Let yourself react, by all means, but once you determine that the stressor isn't dangerous or that it isn't going to continue, bring yourself down with your breathing. No matter where you are or what time it is, breathing is always there for you in a crisis situation. You can rescue yourself at any time. Remember that you are in control here.

DRIVE-BY MEDITATION

Once you've had a chance to halt the initiation of a full-blown stress response, take an opportunity to go deeper into a place of peace. Use mindfulness as a tool to help you reach tranquility; imagine that you can pick up and put down this tool all day long at your own convenience. I call these snippets of meditation "drive-by meditations."

What exactly is a drive-by meditation? Take a few moments, close your eyes, and do a breathing practice where you focus on images of a peaceful place or a source of personal strength. You can do this anywhere, no matter what your day is like. Don't get caught up in the idea that you have to have 20 minutes or a waterfall next to you in order to get the benefits of meditation. In combination with breathing slowly and deeply, the following mindfulness practices will maintain your sense of awareness, centeredness, and clarity, no matter how many balls you have in the air.

Walking Meditation

The walking meditation is often practiced with Buddhism. You can practice this even if you're only walking as far as the restroom in your office building. Use the moments it takes you to walk the length of a hallway to slow things down, breathe, and notice the present. Instead of thinking, focus your attention on the sway of your body as you walk. You can do this while walking down the street or through a room in your house. Just be mindful while you walk.

RETREAT VIA YOUR SENSES

Essential oils go right to the source: the limbic system of your brain. This is where the control boards—the nervous and respiratory systems—for the stress response are located. When feeling stress, your respiration changes, and your nervous system and stress response follow suit. Inhaling an aroma, however, works to distract your limbic system by giving it an opportunity to experience something different. If you deeply and slowly inhale a scent, your nervous system switches gears to move from a sympathetic response into a more parasympathetic response, which will help you change your breathing, relax your muscles, and come back to center.

To get the benefits of aromatherapy, place the oil in a diffuser or rub a drop on your clavicle. Try basil, bergamot, cedarwood, clary sage, cypress, geranium, grapefruit, jasmine, lavender, marjoram, pine, petit grain, rosemary, sandalwood, or ylang-ylang.

YOGA AS A RESCUE TOOL

Performing this simple and stimulating yoga sequence (called a Sun Salutation) can help bring your body/mind connection back to balance after you've experienced acute stress. This sequence will help open the channels of energy required for emotional stability and your physical and mental health. Repeat the sequence at least five times in succession.

S.O.S

MOUNTAIN POSE

Stand tall with your feet together, arms extended down along your sides. Keep a strong foundation with your legs and keep your stomach firm. Reach up tall through your head, looking straight ahead. Breathe deeply and consistently for 5 long breaths.

MOUNTAIN POSE WITH ARMS OVERHEAD

From Mountain Pose, inhale deeply. On the exhalation, raise your arms overhead. Reach your hands up, shoulder-width apart, as high as you can. Don't hunch your shoulders, and do relax your neck. Take 5 long, deep, relaxed breaths.

FORWARD BEND

From Mountain Pose with Arms Overhead, bend your knees slightly. Inhale. On the exhalation, slowly bend forward from your waist while you continue to reach up tall through your arms. Place your hands on the floor alongside your feet or, if you have the flexibility, grasp your ankles. Keep your back straight and your neck soft. Breathe deeply for 5 long breaths.

FORWARD BEND WITH HEAD UP

From the Forward Bend position, inhale deeply. On the exhalation, raise your torso slightly. Reach up through your chest and look straight ahead. Keep your back straight, your neck and shoulders relaxed, and your hands touching the floor alongside or just in front of your toes. Take 5 long, comfortable breaths.

PUSH-UP POSE

Inhale, and as you exhale flatten your hands on the floor and step your feet back behind you, lowering yourself to a push-up position. Hold your torso about 6 inches above the floor. Keep your elbows tight to your body and your stomach strong and firm. Maintain a long, firm body as you gaze down, slightly in front of you. Hold this posture for 5 long, even breaths.

UPWARD FACING DOG

In Push-up Pose, inhale. Exhale, releasing your entire body to the floor. Move your hands alongside your waist, keeping your elbows tight to the sides of your body. Turn your toes back and spread your feet about hip-width apart. Inhale. On the exhalation, pull your trunk forward and raise your head upward, pressing firmly with your hands and fully extending your arms. Keep your legs firm and strong, and lift your knees off the floor. Push your chest forward and up. Hold this posture for 5 long, comfortable breaths.

DOWNWARD FACING DOG

From Upward Facing Dog, bend your elbows and release your torso to the floor. Keep your feet about hip-width apart. Position your hands alongside your chest. Inhale. As you exhale, roll back over your toes, press your palms into the floor, and raise your hips straight up, extending your arms completely. Drop your head toward your feet, pushing back through your hands and straightening your elbows. As you begin to press through your legs and extend back from your arms through your shoulders, your hips will rise to the sky. Relax your neck and release your shoulders back. Hold this posture for 5 long, deep breaths.

FORWARD BEND WITH HEAD UP

From Downward Facing Dog, inhale, bend your knees, and slowly step your feet forward and together between your hands or as close to your hands as possible. Exhale, straightening your legs and placing your hands alongside your feet. Lift your torso and chest so you're looking straight ahead. Keep your back long and supple, your legs strong and stable, and your neck and shoulders relaxed. Hold this posture for 5 long, even breaths.

FORWARD BEND

From Forward Bend with Head Up, inhale. On the exhalation, grasp your ankles with your hands and drop your head toward your knees, gently pulling your torso toward your thighs. Keep your back long and supple, your neck and shoulders relaxed. Hold this posture for 5 long, comfortable breaths.

MOUNTAIN POSE WITH ARMS OVERHEAD

In Forward Bend, inhale deeply. On the exhalation, gracefully raise your torso straight up, reaching your arms overhead and keeping your hands shoulder-width apart, your fingers reaching skyward. Reach as tall as you can. Keep your legs active, your waist long, and lift through your chest. Hold this posture for 5 long, even breaths.

MOUNTAIN POSE

From Mountain Pose with Arms Overhead, inhale. On the exhalation, release your arms down alongside your body, extending your fingers toward the floor. Stand tall with your feet together, keeping your legs active and your stomach firm. Reach up tall through your head, looking straight ahead. Relax your neck and shoulders. Concentrate on lengthening your body and being as tall as you can. Breathe deeply and consistently for 5 long breaths. Release.

SELF-MASSAGE AND ACUPRESSURE

Self-massage and acupressure are good short-term solutions for relieving stress, in that they help your body relax. Acupressure is the oldest form of massage. By asserting pressure with your fingers or hands on specific areas of your body, you release trapped energy that causes various ailments.

Maintaining a Positive Energy Flow

Acute stress can cause your body to lose energy really fast. To help relieve acute stress and maintain a positive flow of energy throughout your body, use this treatment a few times a day.

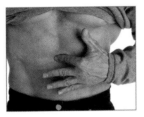

You can perform this technique standing or sitting. Place your forefinger and middle finger about 2 inches above your navel. Begin to gently apply pressure to this area. Work your fingers in a small circular motion, increasing pressure on the area as you become used to the sensation. Work into the area for 10 deep, consistent breaths, release, and repeat 2 or 3 times. Make sure to keep your breathing relaxed.

Relieving Day-to-Day Stress

Practice this simple massage for quick and effective stress relief.

You can perform this treatment while standing or sitting. Maintain an erect spine while performing the massage—don't hunch your shoulders or slouch. Keep your chest up and your shoulders relaxed so you can breathe deeply and comfortably. Using both hands, reach to the back of your neck, placing your fingers on either side at the base of your skull. Gently press with each hand into the base of your neck. As you start to relax, exert more pressure on both sides of your neck. Massage the area until you feel relief, breathing comfortable and deeply the entire time.

Index

Underscored page references indicate boxed text and photograph captions. **Boldface** references indicate photographs.

Turn the tables on stress with *Health Solutions for Stress Relief*

Proven relief from the negative feelings and health effects of stress is now in your own hands.

This advanced, total-health approach restores healthy mind-body responses to stress through simple yet powerful nutrition, relaxation techniques, insights on setting up your internal and external environments, and more. You'll feel your energy levels increase, your sources of stress become more manageable, and your resilience to stress grow stronger—so you can take stress in stride and handle it with focus, confidence, and ease.

- Guide you through simple relaxation techniques so you can reclaim your calm fast
- Demonstrate easy exercises that release tension and rebalance stress hormones
- Give you simple workout and relaxation tools with powerful stress-relief effects
- Show you clinically proven solutions that can be customized to your lifestyle

Health Solutions for Stress Relief DVD

Turn stress into a positive source of energy by giving your body what it needs for its natural, healthy stress-management processes. Dr. James Rouse helps you identify your sources of stress and reactions to stress and shows you how to use guided relaxation, breathing exercises, self-massage, and other simple techniques to release tension in minutes. Restorative yoga demonstrated by renowned yoga master Rodney Yee helps you feel in control of stress every day. Includes 16-page guidebook with frequently asked questions, stress-remedy checklist, reference list of stress-busting foods, and 7-day menu with recipes. 1 hour 40 minutes.

Health Solutions— A.M. Stress Relief Kit

This easy-to-use kit helps you start your day feeling vibrant, focused, and prepared for anything. Dr. James Rouse guides you through a quick, revitalizing A.M. resistance-band workout, and three included resistance bands with increasing levels of resistance help build stress resilience. A helpful guide offers tips on rejuvenating with included A.M. Stress Relief aromatherapy oil, plus insight on stress-management nutrition, a sample recipe for a stress-prevention breakfast, and an overview of how exercise can help bolster your resilience to stress as you begin each day.

Health Solutions for Stress Relief Travel Kit

A hectic travel schedule, a stressful day at work . . . Want to keep stress in check? Quickly create a calming environment and glide through the tension with this convenient go-anywhere kit. On audio CD, Dr. James Rouse guides you through calming relaxation and breathing techniques followed by tranquil instrumental music to help your mind and body rebalance. A unique adjustable, inflatable neck pillow with therapeutic weights targets key acupressure points to help release physical tension. You also get a travel-size bottle of calming Stress Relief Travel Blend aromatherapy oil plus a better-sleep travel guide with aromatherapy tips and recipes for an on-the-go stress-balancing snack.

Health Solutions— P.M. Stress Relief Kit

Release the day's tension and unwind more easily with this practical evening kit. Dr. James Rouse guides you through a simple 15-minute yoga practice using the included mini restorative yoga bolster to release physical tension, calm your mind, and restore a feeling of balance. A helpful guide offers tips on soothing your senses with included P.M. Stress Relief aromatherapy oil, plus insight on stress-management nutrition, a sample recipe for a stress-balancing evening meal, and an overview of how exercise can help you get through hectic days.

James Rouse holds a doctorate in naturopathic medicine from National College in Portland, Oregon, the oldest accredited naturopathic medical school in the nation. "Dr. James" is also a certified yoga instructor and integrated health expert, with a multidisciplinary background that includes psychology and post-doctorate training and study in acupuncture, Chinese medicine, and Tibetan Ayurvedic medicine. In addition to heading a busy private practice, Dr. James hosts wellness news and related radio and television programs across the United States.

THE ART OF LIVING IN HARMONY
with
YOURSELF AND YOUR WORLD

GAIAM®